AF486514

A PORTAL TO EARTH ENERGY

The Path of the Gridworker

By Dr. Kenzie Ann Rhodes, DD

All rights reserved. Neither this book nor any parts within it may be sold or reproduced in any format by any electronic or mechanical means including information storage and retrieval systems without written permission from the author. The only exception is by a reviewer, who may quote short excerpts in a review.

Other books by the same author:
Crystal Grid Fairies- A Young Lightworker's Guide
Series, and Missions
Published by Azuray Productions;
Hampden County on Massachusetts
Copyright © 2023 by Kenzie Rhodes

TABLE OF CONTENTS

INTRODUCTION

It has been said that proof of God's existence can be found simply by stepping out into Nature. Presence exists in every blade of grass, every bird's song, every whisper of wind; all of which are expressions of the Divine manifesting here on Earth. Our glorious planet Is not just a thing, a commodity to be carved up and owned. She is a living entity with consciousness of her own, and a Divine template that mirrors our own.

The history of the human collective is intimately connected to the history of Earth. Science and religion have worked diligently for hundreds, perhaps thousands, of years to convince us that we are small and limited and that our planet is small and limited. Through a control grid of public education and media, they have been successful in reducing the cosmic awesomeness down to a sum of its parts, wrapping mainstream conclusions in language designed to limit the imagination and deny the

cosmic truths that often are found through clair-
cognizance. This inner knowing, coming in through the
third eye as if downloaded, is what orthodox religions
describe as communication from Holy Spirit.

A spiritual awakening; the rising of
consciousness is happening to the family of man living
here on and within Earth as we move slowly through the
photon belt in our galaxy and are bombarded by plasma
light codes. As consciousness rises, long hidden truths
are being revealed. Ancient memories contained within
our fragmented DNA are resurfacing; the so-called
"junk" that mainstream science dismisses as irrelevant
are awakening within us while the DNA of Earth herself
is also awakening along galactic grid lines. There have
been and continue to be many revelations: the ordered,
mathematical perfection of the Universe, sacred
geometry, which is mirrored in our own organic
blueprint, and in the organic blueprint of the Earth itself.
As our personal consciousness dances along meridians
and emanates as energies from chakras, or energy

vortices of our physical bodies, Earth's energies and consciousness dance along grid lines and emanate from the vortices of her physical body. Our carbon-to-diamond forms are made up of the same carbon-to-diamond materials of which the Earth is composed; symbiosis is evident.

As we are waking up to the realization of our own multi-dimensionality and its relevance to our ascension, so must we recognize that the same is true of our home; Earth, and that we have a great responsibility as her stewards. Along with the recognition of who and what she truly is comes our requirement to take right action in a Sacred and Divine mission toward her healing and protection as her Stewards, and we have the map which shows us the way forward.

The map is not set in stone, but it evolves as we chart our course forward, testing each step and listening with open ears to the communication that she shares with us.

This book serves several purposes. First, it is a demonstration of the sameness of the energetic blueprint which is shared by Earth and humans; thus, we may apply the same principles of health and healing that we use for ourselves to her.

Second, it provides a very basic historical context for the reader to begin recognizing how an overlay of illusion has kept humanity enslaved for time immemorial. A truth, once known, can never be unknown and this clarity empowers us with the much-needed discernment to withdraw our consent from these systems and to discontinue participating in actions that cause further harm.

Finally, it is meant to inspire awakening gridworkers to begin working actively and intentionally with Earth Energies, armed with a rudimentary baseline understanding. It is a clarion call and a guide for action.

When I began to feel called toward gridworking, I searched endlessly for resources that would help me, and found nothing that was both practical and comprehensive. The subject is so vast that it can be overwhelming. It incorporates deep esoteric wisdom, alchemy and practice. I wanted to create something that would help others who find themselves on a similar path. This book is meant to provide a basic blueprint for actualization; a launchpad, so to speak.

This work combines the esoteric with the scientific and presents some resources that will help the reader to dig further into research and practices that appeal to him or her. The greater that we expand our awareness, the more that we grow into our own multi-dimensionality. Much knowing comes with practice, and the biggest barrier is often simply a lack of trust in the self's innate knowing what to do. By far the most important thing is intention, and the motivation to begin. Stepping out of the mental and into the physical through action is the actualization of intention, and this is where the power lies. The secret is to just roll up your sleeves and begin.

CHAPTER ONE: AWAKENING ON A FAST-TRACK

I came to the realization that my mission here on Earth was something beyond the mainstream when I met someone who I thought was my twin flame in the Spring of 2021. Turns out, it was an activation contract and not the timeless bond of twin flames, nevertheless at the time I had never heard the terms "twin flame" or even "grid-worker" before. I was not particularly drawn to crystals or overly interested in actually doing energy healing. I had just purchased a Rife machine and was beginning to learn about sound frequency and its effects on health. I was also unhappily working in a matrix job, chasing dollars. The spiritual activations began coming in fast and furious, propelling me forward on a wild ride that I could never have begun to imagine possible. My clair-cognition took center stage, and one after another, synchronicities began to blow up every area of my life. I began experiencing spiritual downloads, knowing things without knowing how I knew. Both my inner and my outer landscapes began to change; a process that would have me looking back on and realizing that I no longer even resembled that person that I had believed myself to be for more than half of a century.

A growing sense of responsibility was transforming my entire outlook, and it began with the responsibility to know myself fully. This forced me to prioritize my own journey of healing and growth; spiritual, emotional, mental and physical. It grew into an awareness that I needed to actively do something to benefit not only humanity, but the Earth as well. I didn't know what that was going to look like exactly. What I did know was that whatever it was would not include doing what I had always done; giving my life energy to a job that I hated and which was serving no one. I was meant to be something completely different. I could feel it, but I couldn't put my finger on it. I was being forced to learn patience throughout all of 2022, as I doggedly practiced mindfulness and spiritual discipline, and worked at actively healing all the different levels of my energetic and physical self. In retrospect, I know beyond the shadow of a doubt that being activated to the so-called "twin flame journey" was the triggering event.

This book is not about so contracts, soul mates, or the twin flame phenomenon; which in the last several years has birthed an entire industry. Many Tarot readers and spiritual counselors have built thriving online businesses with large communities of people seeking answers and even simple validation of their shared experiences in this unusual relationship dynamic that has a distinctly other- worldly quality to it. There are many different soul contracts, and the focus should be on the internal transformation that they are meant to trigger. However, many people stay focused on the dynamic itself, rather than on personal growth and the work that the experience is meant to catalyze. People have many different explanations of the true purpose of the twin flame incarnation, and in all probability each twin flame couple has a journey that is every bit as unique as the individual soul journey. I am a twin flame, but my counterpart was not that person, and when my true Divine Masculine came home to me, I suddenly understood. My experience on the Awakening path has been one of exponential soul growth, and I was catapulted to heights that I had never previously even dreamed of. I turned my back on a well-paying career that I had spent decades building, because it was not feeding my spirit and was draining me of vital life force. I was no longer satisfied with life in the matrix. There was something much more out there for me. My soul was yearning ever forward and upward, reaching for that enormous purpose that it had come here to fulfill and to help me remember what I needed to remember.

In the summer, the call of a beautiful citrine Vogel crystal ignited my awakening to the recognition of my specific purpose. From there, I began exploring crystals and what they can do and delved into Earth's crystal caves and their purpose. I had been very drawn to the idea of star gates and ascension mechanics since I had stumbled upon old information sources that introduced galactic history and Keylontic Science, and so my interest in the Earth's energetic blueprint was a natural result and progression of these discoveries.

In October of 2022, I instinctively began using geometrical patterns to plant crystal grids in various locations out in nature around the towns near where I live, and I also began experimenting with remote gridwork; inviting like-minded friends to participate. Almost immediately, synchronicities started to happen. Cloud portals formed in the sky above the lands where the grids were planted, followed by the appearance of brightly colored orbs above the trees on our family land. In a short time, a matter of days, everything took on a very personal significance when I suddenly began receiving messages through very vivid dreams, which confirmed my role here as a protector of Earth's grid. I learned of my soul lineage as a Guardian of the Blue Flame, which is one of the first Emanations of Creation. As I began actively doing in-person gridwork and facilitating remote gridwork missions, more and more signs and synchronicities showed me that I was on the right path. Unexpectedly, the opportunity to resurrect an old university degree program that I had started and then abandoned more than a decade year prior suddenly presented itself. This time, I was able to complete my doctoral dissertation and receive the degree. It turned out that the school had gotten accredited sometime during all the years that I had been away. What was once very much alternative had made it into the mainstream. I was also able to revisit and master several energy healing modalities that I had dabbled in, in the past, and I began to apply myself consciously to do healing work with people and animals.

Sometimes the healing that is going on is so deep that you are unaware that it is happening. As I was waiting for my dissertation to be reviewed, I suddenly realized that the writer's block that had plagued me for decades had melted away. I had managed to get a master's culminating project and an entire dissertation completed in a matter of weeks. Suddenly, there was nothing stopping me from writing. And so, I began pouring everything that I had into creating; including books and guides for children. I wanted to help young lightworkers learn about Earth Energy, healing and developing their gifts. It was becoming clearer and clearer that there was a need to help guide the younger ones along this path. I had spent a lifetime struggling to find my way, and now I could be a lighthouse for others. The Crystal Grid Fairies Series was born.

The many months since (eighteen at the that I first wrote this) have been a time of completing cycles, of deep study and integration, and of creation. Learning all that I can about our planetary mother, doing the work to protect and strengthen her, and teaching others has become an important part of my life, and I am truly grateful for this sacred mission here in this incarnation. I welcome all other grid workers and awakening spiritual teachers, and celebrate our shared journey here, in Service to Others, and in Service to the Land.

CHAPTER TWO: CONNECTION TO THE LAND

Nature expresses the consciousness of life, and recognition of this is felt across the organic lands of every continent, where the evidence of Earth Energies reveals itself in the landmarks and pathways. It can also be found within the ancestral memories of the peoples living in and around the regions; in the stories about their history, their cultural celebrations and practices, and embedded within the group consciousness of the populations. Recognition of and reverence for it are hinted at in myths and legends surrounding a certain ruin, an outcropping of rocks, mountains, and burial sites, as well as other places commonly found in nature. It is felt in the brush of a cool air current, in the heavy stillness that recognizes the solemn weight of history, in the welcoming sanctuary of a sacred grove, and in the breath-stealing sense of awe at a mighty waterfall or some other majestic expression of nature. It can be heard in the voices of animals who call out from these sacred places, and in the silence of other areas where no animals choose to go near. Some ancient instinct whispers to us that something is there, even when we can't see it with our physical eyes.

The lack of Earth Energy is also felt profoundly. It is very evident in cities, where the artificial and the man-made have completely blocked the flow of Nature and have imbued a facade of anti-life consciousness into the populations who live there. Disconnection from Nature is disconnection from Source, and the asphalt jungles and other artificial places where man has cast out God are dead zones that bring down consciousness of all life existing therein and even spread like a blight out into the surrounding lands. People who live in cities teeming with never-ending activity insist the energy they find there amidst others who are like-minded has a unique and exciting life-force that is palpable. This may very well be true; however, it is the creative life-force of all the other humans living there who are sustaining that excitement and cycling it back into the collective even as the artificial life is fed and grows. The land itself is unable to give or to receive. As time passes and people remain in these areas without replenishing their connection to Earth, and to Source, that which was once organic gradually becomes more and more artificial and focused on the external. Intrinsic values that the human race has shared since time immemorial begin to erode as each generation is more disconnected than the previous. And humans are infinitely resourceful and fluid. With time, we adjust to incoherence as normalcy and because it feels familiar and "safe", we seek it out not realizing how much better coherence would be. We truly don't know what we don't know.

The replacement of organic with the artificial is a slow process that has been happening for a very long time. The deliberate placement of man-made structures intruding onto sites of Earth power speaks to conscious awareness of their significance and potential. It also speaks to deliberate intent. Churches, temples, tombs, monuments, pyramids and other architectural structures are very often built in these locations, covering up evidence from the local (Native) populations that may have been there first. Sacred places are commodified and defiled by commercialism. Tourism replaces pilgrimage, and in the blink of an eye, the profane has taken over the sacred. Military forts and commemorative statues are erected over places where historical events took place; locking the distorted archetypal energies of authoritarianism, control and war into the land. Chevrons and signs detail and mark important historical sites which may have changed beyond all recognition. And even without man's attempts to lay human claim to these emotionally charged areas, still the land holds the memories in the form of energies in her body; just as we humans hold in our unconscious minds and our biofield blueprints the memories of what has happened to us, and emotions we have felt.

There remains much to learn and discover about Earth, and still an odyssey to weave together from the patchwork quilt of perspectives and stories of all people of the world. This is not only the story of Earth, but also the story of humanity. There are many ways that pieces of this story come to us, ways that go well beyond the boundaries of "science"; a framework that has been built upon limitation and reductionist thinking. This method completely ignores (and even actively denies the existence of) our other non-physical senses, only focusing on the five senses that connect to the material, three-dimensional world. Too many people follow this religion without even realizing that they are worshiping in much the same way as do the adherents of formal religious paths.

We are observers of planetary energies as grid workers, we pluck information from the ethers in the unseen realms psychically as remote viewers. We access long dormant memories and travel to different dimensions and lifetimes in our dreams. We discover natural and manmade vortices and star gates, and reverse star gates. We detect and decode holographic energy structures, living energy, dead energy; differentiating

what energies and consciousnesses are there. And we are
not alone in the recognition of what is imprinted upon
the land. Crop circles (Deane, 2002, p 187-188) are one
way that extraterrestrial beings "code' the land with
frequencies, transmitted using the language of sacred
geometry. Our galactic star families communicate more
overtly with Earth than they do with us, it seems. In his
book, *Earth's Forbidden Secrets, Part I*, author and
researcher Maxwell Igan describes numerous other
examples of ways in which past civilizations native to
Earth and galactic visitors have left evidence of their
presence in many locations including Egypt and Africa.
(Igan, 2010). Now, as we move through 2023, we find
that a great many hidden truths have already begun to
rise to the surface of the collective consciousness. The
veil has begun to dissolve as evidence demonstrates that
a "Great Awakening" is well and truly underway.

What the masses have for many years considered
to be Truth is slowly being turned inside out by
mainstream science, revealing itself to be merely the

outer limits of a frequency fence. The children of the West, particularly those of us who have been born into these recent generations of North American society, have grown up immersed in the religion of science, which has been taught as separate and distinct from worship of actual "religion"; although they are truly one in the same. We have been taught to choose between two very structured polarities which appear to be at war with each other, and the liberal versus conservative ideologies stand out strongly in our identities as "reality".

Interestingly, Eastern fundamental philosophy down through the ages has always recognized that ideologies are a construct. The world which we perceive is *maya*, according to ancient Hindu wisdom; illusion. Science pays no attention to ancient wisdom, and it can only prevail in a culture of control and censorship. Its structured, boxed-in thinking demands rigid adherence to very specific narratives and dogmas, all of which ensure the continued status and financial success of the scientists while at the same time minimizing Nature's power. In *The View Over Atlantis,* Michell observes "scientific facts emerge in the first instance as revelations from the unconscious mind. Where these revelations can be shown to accord with what has already been established, they are accepted. Where they stand alone, they tend to be dismissed as fantasies, even though to certain people they are more real than the system which they appear to contradict." (Michell, 1975, p 21). Over the course of the last several decades, this rigid thinking has devolved into something that now resembles a full-blown religion. Indeed, the term "scientism" describes the belief that the only truth is that which comes from scientific methods. This belief system contradicts the very existence of human potential.

In recent history, mystics, scientists, and other abstract thinkers who have stepped forward with information and evidence that contradicts prevailing zeitgeist have been dubbed heretics by the established "experts" and dealt with harshly. Many of them, increasingly those born in the 20th century, have had their inventions, blueprints and intellectual property either stolen or destroyed. Walter Russell, Nicola Tesla, Max Gerson, Ignaz Semmelweis, Stanley Meyer, Aries DeGeus, Eugene Mallove, and Andrew Moulden are but a few examples of trailblazers who pushed the boundaries of the current naradigm. All were many years ahead of their own time, and they each helped to forge a new pathway through the fire toward increasingly higher levels of consciousness of the collective.

We are currently living in a time where disclosure is happening, and the limited little bubble of perception understood by humanity has been slowly shrinking. The ancient civilizations of Hyperborea, Tartaria, Atlantis and Lemuria were once dismissed as myths; they are now being discussed and referenced, as more and more people become open to history that has been buried and hidden. More and more people are also realizing that they feel a personal connection to these civilizations; some small spark of awareness becomes triggered when we are exposed to information that presents something different. The triggering is ancient cellular memory awakening and beginning to come online, moving from the depths of the subconscious into the conscious mind. Because the population has been conditioned to dismiss knowledge that does not register by way of the physical senses, we have a hard time recognizing the awakening process for what it is. Many of us have learned through experiences of our solitary journeys, with no teacher or guide other than the one within. Many of us have had these experiences ever since we were little, when we quickly learned to suppress our inner knowing so to be accepted by a three-dimensional society that has not valued our uniqueness. Imagination has been pooh-poohed by the mainstream public education system, dismissed as fanciful rather than recognized as the human gift that it is. Children who display too much imagination have even been targeted by the medical control system as "sick" and find themselves suppressed with poisonous drugs to shut down and block their natural abilities and awareness.

This is a great tragedy that our recent generations have had to suffer.

Interestingly, Service-to-self consciousnesses themselves unknowingly contributed to humanity's Great Awakening by their own actions during their pandemic of 2020. By abruptly departing from insistence that truth can only be found where it can be evidenced in the physical world to demanding that all physical evidence being seen, heard or felt be ignored "unless the experts tell you otherwise", a cognitive pendulum was set in motion, swinging back and forth to shake people out of their old, rigid belief systems.

The intentions were to manufacture a state of confusion by sending incoherent and conflicting messages, creating what is known in hypnotherapy and neuro linguistic programming circles as a doorway into the unconscious mind. When the door opens, subliminal messages can slip past someone's awareness into the unconscious mind and take root. This is the way that phobias and limiting beliefs are formed. The Service-to-self controllers intended to mass-hypnotize the entire world in those moments and install their New World Order programs, however this backfired significantly for a portion of the population and instead woke them up. The polarized rocking back and forth of opposing beliefs created a holistic phenomenon that shook a great many people out of their previous, unawake and unaware state.

This is one of the methods utilized by Hale Dwoskin, a contemporary of Lester Levinson, the founder of Sedona Method. The method, a simple yet elegant system of emotional self-healing developed in the 1950s, is based on the conscious choice to let go of emotional blocks. The method's philosophy rests upon the recognition that all attachments stem from just four human needs; approval, security, control, or separation. The method teaches several different processes for releasing attachment to outcomes, both real and perceived. One of the techniques that it uses is called holistic releasing, which works actively with polarized ideas and beliefs, taking the person back and forth between the two polarities. This process has the powerful effect of shaking cognitive dissonance loose and allowing attachment to fear-based outcomes to drop away, resulting in emotional freedom. (Dwoskin, 2007). A belief that attachment is the root of all human suffering is also one of the core tenets of traditional schools of Buddhism.

This mass awakening that began in 2020 has been greatly aided by an overall increase in the collective level of consciousness that many people here on Earth have noticed and felt profoundly. This is directly tied to the cosmos and has been happening organically as Earth moves through the photon belt. Gradually, the sun's intensity has been growing, releasing higher frequencies with light codes in each plasma filled solar wave. Psychic awareness and abilities are beginning to come online in greater numbers of people, who are now questioning everything that they have ever been taught. Hidden history is coming to light, showing us a completely different past than what we learned in school.

Dirty secrets about agendas and deliberate harm to the population are no longer buried and are coming out into the light of day for all to see.

With each system that we look at, we find behind it increasing levels of control, manipulation, and coercion. We find that our education system has been dumbing us down and hiding true history, that our medical system is making us addicted to chemicals and chronically sick, that our politicians have been controlling us, and that our food systems are serving us nutritionally bankrupt, processed meals. Society has been deliberately steered into a state of mindless compliance and consumption, and this has been going on for hundreds, perhaps thousands of years. As the frequencies of Earth and the sun continue to rise, those things which are not of the new, higher frequencies begin to crumble and fall away in the Great Awakening. And everywhere, people are finding others who are like-minded, and coming together in online and physical communities and groups, building strong connections based on common ground and shared information. This phenomenon continues to pick up speed and momentum as we move forward, and more and more people begin to heed the call of the Divine and look to a more spiritual path.

CHAPTER THREE: MULTI –DIMENSIONAL

Gnosis must be used necessary to piece together the many different dimensions that make up our full comprehension of who and what we are as humans. The same is true of our recognition of Earth. This great being, both densely physical and intuitively energetic, is so many things; a spot on the star map, a sanctuary and a refuge, and a library which hosts and contains timelines full of ancient histories that are vast, linear and cyclical. Earth is truly multi-dimensional, and awareness of multi-dimensional consciousness is necessary to see her Divine blueprint, and all that she is. The old one- and two-dimensional ways of thinking, embodied in the current mainstream understanding of what "science" is, will no longer suffice for those whose awareness has already begun to expand. Just as many are beginning to reject the limited thinking that has kept us in ignorance of our own history and our connection to each other and to Source, they are also realizing how limited we have been in our perceptions of our planet.

The evidence that these things are happening is all around us for those with eyes to see and ears to hear. As the frequency fences holding humanity trapped in lower states of consciousness through inverted control systems are slowly crumbling, more and more people are walking away from old identities and stepping onto spiritual paths that feed their souls. A new way of thinking is emerging; one that is not dependent upon external validation from institutional sources, but instead relies upon inner knowing. Part of that inner knowing is the recognition that all of us are united in a universal and collective desire for peace, harmony, equality, authenticity, love and freedom. Despite the attempts by subversive forces to keep us focused on differences by highlighting superficial qualities and declaring them all-important, humanity as a whole is seeing through the illusions, and is beginning to refuse to keep playing the games. This "divide and conquer" method worked well in the past to keep the masses trapped in the density of lower states of consciousness, but it is no longer working. It cannot be sustained in the new, higher frequencies.

We are becoming more conscious; realizing that our willing participation in our own enslavement has enabled the systems of tyranny and control to keep us separate from each other and disconnected from Source for a very long time. Unitive consciousness, a hallmark of the Law of One, is a recognition of the multi-dimensionality of Source as it is expressed within all things. Tapping into this high level of connection is a way to bring us into our hearts and allows us to feel the unity of oneness with all other beings. (Ra. 1984). This connection is our Divine birthright, and it is time for us to reclaim it. For far too long, we have lived within an ego-controlled construct of the lower chakras, moving further and further away from love, responsibility and connection with each other. The lower chakras are focused more upon the self and the physical body, as they connect us to the material world and to survival.

A disconnection from the outwardly expanding consciousness of the higher chakras is the only way that an angelic human being would ever entertain the idea that artificial augmentation of the organic body is desirable or superior to the organic. Unfortunately, those who travel this path do not even realize that they have become completely disconnected from Source. Many of them do not remember a time when they were ever connected; matrix conditioning is already at work trying to shut down human consciousness even when it is in the womb.

There are so many ways that this disconnection shows itself; messages coming from Spirit as it tries to get the attention of the person. The disconnection makes itself known through depression, anxiety and other mental health-related conditions. It expresses itself in behavioral problems. It comes through in physical ailments and diseases. Disconnection; spiritual bankruptcy, is the true root cause of every imaginable pain felt by humanity. The natural result of higher states of consciousness is the movement into heart-centered focus that is plugged directly into the Divine current, and with that rise comes the deliberate and intentional rejection of anything that is artificial, synthetic and anti-life.

This is not to imply that the lower chakras are somehow negative or responsible for one's lack of discernment or disconnection from Source. Humans have a physical body and are meant to experience the physical world through that physical body and the lower chakras make it possible. It is exceedingly important that a regular practice of healing and balancing is maintained to keep the chakras free from distortions, entities and implants. A spiritually embodied individual has an energy blueprint that is balanced and integrated through all the chakras; this in turn balances the auric system which emanates from the chakras.

Earth is conscious and has a physical body; just as all beings that inhabit her are conscious and have physical bodies. She is also so much more. She appears as a dense concentration of many frequencies of sound and light that make up physical matter, as does anything that is perceptible to our five physical senses. She has chakras; vortexes that concentrate specific archetypal energies and meridians upon which these energies flow, and she has specific, organic architecture contained on and within her body. She is a combination of both the electric and the magnetic, as are we. "Like the energies of the human body, the spirit of earth flows through the surface in channels or veins, and between the two energy currents of man and earth there exists a natural affinity. "(Michell, 1975, p12).

Earth also contains technologies and structures that have been deliberately implanted in and upon her body by humans and nonhuman entities, of both Service - to-self and Service-to-others perspectives, to utilize and tap into her energies. These energy sources are vast, and they are immensely powerful. Depending upon the intentions of the architects, these implants may either be for the benefit of life and of Earth, or for their detriment.

Similar to the way that dis-ease processes can afflict humans, animals and plants, the Earth also experiences di-ease; and as with all beings, this can worsen or heal with intention and focused action. Blocked energy patterns can become locked into physical form, and with time they will result in physical ailments that eventually express themselves in the three-dimensional reality. In the immortal words of Nicola Tesla, "if you want to find the secrets of the universe, think in terms of energy, frequency and vibration." Everything is energy, and this holds as true for Earth as it does for our own bodies.

Recognition of a human biofield, a pattern of energy surrounding the body, was given mainstream voice in 1994 by the National Institute of Health. Eileen Day Mckusick, a pioneer in the then newly emerging science of the biofield, explains "there is indeed a sort of magnetic fluid surrounding and interpenetrating the body, and blockages in this field are representations of blockages within the body. Where energy does not flow, pathologies arise." (Mckusick, 2021, p 109). Another holistic practitioner, Dr. Bradley Nelson, credited with the development of the Emotion Code and the Body Code energy healing techniques, describes how the energetic movement patterns of emotion create vibrations which are felt within the body, then released (processed). The body is designed to be a filtering tool, and this is the natural flow of emotional energies. However, when emotions are not released, either because they are deliberately suppressed or interrupted, then that energy becomes stuck, and often lodges itself somewhere inside the cells of that person's body. "Trapped emotions actually consist of well-defined energies that have a shape and form. Although they are not visible, they are very real." (Nelson, 2019, p 7).

These trapped emotions can cause endless suffering, and very often the suffering individual cannot even consciously remember what the triggering event that caused the problem was. The unconscious mind, however, remembers everything and Nelson's technique taps into the knowledge held in the unconscious to find and release these energy blockages from the body. Once something comes into conscious awareness, it can then be healed. A truth, once known, can never again be unknown. This is why journeys of the spiritual must involve seeing and acknowledging the darkness to consciously choose a different path. A common mistake that many students of the "new age" make is to avoid anything that they consider negative; this is a form of spiritual bypassing, because clarity requires contrast. Lack of clarity is a huge contributor to the unconscious manifesting that humans have been engaged in to create the unpleasant realities that are being revealed to us now on the world stage. A great deal has been written and spoken about this, and one of the hallmarks of a true spiritual teacher is the willingness to acknowledge darkness. In the words of Anis Springate; "the ability to hold light is directly proportional to the courage to see darkness." This is necessary for effective healing and advancement along the path toward spiritual mastery.

In the last sixty years at least, more and more pioneers of energy healing methods have brought their discoveries forward and enjoyed finding acceptance in the mainstream consciousness by an increasingly more open-minded population. Gary Craig is credited with popularizing Emotional Freedom Technique; finger-tapping on specific points on the body that correspond to the body's meridians. He was developing and perfecting his research in the early 1990's and actively working to help people in his practice. The technique grew out of an earlier body of knowledge known as Thought Field Therapy (TFT) that was used effectively by psychologist Roger Callahan in his practice. Emotional and physical conditions become stuck in the physical body, eventually resulting in health conditions that manifest over time and remain there unless the person can find a way to release the blockages and allow the energy to once more begin flowing freely. Callahan successfully integrated the concepts of energy, frequency and vibration into traditional, mainstream therapy in a manner that created a much greater, holistic healing experience for those who sought his help. A similar evolution began when Richard Bandler and John Grinder began to integrate patterns of behavior with the tools of accessing the subconscious with classical hypnotherapy to successfully help people to rewire their brains in an entirely new way through Neuro Linguistic Programming techniques. The power of humans lies in our ability to create, and each individual human has his own unique gift.

These are just several of the many, many rapidly growing integrative disciplines that have been taking the alternative healing community by storm, and many of the healing modalities are not actually new. Some share roots with religious traditions, such as Buddhism, Taoism and Hinduism, and some integrate ancient practice-based traditions. Ayurveda, for example, is an system of natural healing based upon energy-flow principles that has been practiced by Eastern civilizations for thousands of years. It has been gaining global popularity in the current age, as more and more people have begun to experience concrete benefits from it.

Many techniques, both old and new, are evolving into a wide range of methods which also include Quantum Healing, Theta Healing, and many, more specialized therapies. The root of each of these methods is the same; recognition that energy, frequency and vibration are at the core of all existence here on the planet. If this is true for life upon the Earth, it stands to reason that the same principles will apply to the Earth herself.

Energies have a concrete physical manifestation here on the Earth plane. Blocked energy also becomes lodged in the Earth's body, and the effects of this can be felt in the consciousness field of the beings who live on and near the sources of these blockages. Animals are able to instinctively recognize the energetic patterns that appear in nature, and they naturally gravitate towards, or away from, certain areas. Plentiful food sources in a particular location are a physical sign of an energetic signature gathered there. This phenomenon has been widely acknowledged as truth for many thousands of years by spiritually aware populations. An example of one of the oldest spiritual traditions that recognizes Earth Energy patterns and integrates them into mindful living is Feng Shui.

The foundation of this ancient Eastern tradition, identified by teacher and scholar Kenneth S. Cohen as one of the seven schools of Taoism, rests upon recognition of the subtle effects of energies on the environment. Land masses, natural landmarks, concentrations of elements (water, wood, metal, crystal, and earth, for example) as well as man-made architectures produce verifiable effects on all life that is in the vicinity of these things. Feng Shui utilizes energy signatures to both actively manipulate the environment to achieve desired outcomes, and passively to take advantage of beneficial energies that are being generated naturally.

The same principles of energy apply regardless of whether something is organic from Nature, or a man-made architecture. Good Feng Shui practitioners use their awareness to intentionally maximize beneficial energies in and around a home or a business, while minimizing the deleterious effects, and an entire international industry has grown out of the practice of this knowledge. A recognition of energy flow, and the fundamentals of sacred geometry lie at the core of the deepest teachings of Feng Shui, as does the ability to instinctively feel into the currents of energy flowing within a particular location. Feng Shui practitioners work actively with Earth Energy and have done so for at least the last thirty-five hundred years.

As humans slowly return to the realization that we are stewards of the Earth, and that our actions have consequences that go far beyond the effects of our own personal lives, conscious awareness may be brought forth with intention to reconnect with her, and to help by actively participating in her healing process. When this begins, magic really can start to happen. It is no surprise that Biblical scripture has noted humanity's sacred responsibility to the Earth and all creatures; this ancient knowledge has been carried down through the oral traditions of countless indigenous peoples who still retain Earth Energy awareness.

Our ascension process is described extensively in the Voyagers Series by Ashayana Deane as both spiritual and biological and is intricately connected to Earth. "Spirituality" is simply the portion of true, universal science that (we) do not yet understand, for science is truly the Mechanics of Consciousness and its manifestations, and consciousness is the true spiritual essence of the universe, and all life forms contained within it." (Deane, 2002, p 171). Extensive study of the Tree of Life is presented within the scope of Keylontic Science and is a deep dive into the multidimensionality of ascension. Both the Earth and the original, twelve stranded-DNA angelic humans share the same twelve sphere biological and energetic blueprint, and the sacred number twelve can be found repeated in the physical world, and embedded within the framework of many fundamental teachings, both esoteric and traditional. Pattern recognition soon becomes automatic and aids our gnosis to discern the difference between what is being presented as natural but is actually inverted. This is how people can feel a vague sort of discomfort somewhere in their bodies when looking at something that is artificial, manipulative or negative without being able to consciously identify the root of the unease. Unfortunately, Service-to-self controllers have taught people to ignore their own inner guidance system. With time, this practice of deliberate suppression dulls the innate abilities, and people fall further and further under the spell of the false matrix.

Everything is energy and can be perceived based upon levels of consciousness. The higher that we rise in our individual consciousness, the more we can help to raise the consciousness of others around us; David R. Hawkins, author of *Power Versus Force* has noted that a single avatar consciousness, such as was embodied in Jesus, carries such a powerful frequency that it can influence millions of people who are stuck in apathy, fear or anger. Hawkins writes that if "only fifteen per cent of the world's population is above the critical consciousness level of 200, the collective power of that fifteen per cent has the ability to counterbalance the remaining eighty-five per cent of the world's population." (Hawkins, 1995, p 226). The higher that we rise in our individual consciousness, the more we can help to raise the consciousness of others around us. Hawkins further notes that one human at an enlightened consciousness of 1000 can counterbalance the entire family of man. (Hawkins, 1995, p 226). This is the exponential power of the scale of consciousness; the reason why Jesus, Buddha, and other high consciousness beings had such a profound influence on so many people that their messages continue to reverberate down through the passages of linear time. It explains how a single Joan of Arc, a single King Arthur, a single Martin Luther King, Jr. and a single Gandhi were so effective in influencing the outcome of conflicts against seemingly insurmountable odds. It also explains why a small fraction of the population of America at the time of the Revolutionary War was able to eventually influence the outcome and bring about the birth of a new country with principles based on Freedom. On the consciousness scale, freedom vibrates at the same level as truth. Single individuals with consciousness levels that exceed even three hundred fifty, the level of acceptance, can counterbalance the negativity of millions of people who are stuck in apathy, fear or anger. (Hawkins, 1995, p 220-227).

Lower frequency consciousnesses are not able to directly impact beings with these higher states of consciousness, so parasitic entities look for indirect ways to tear them down by manipulating the tools of influence that belong to the three-dimensional world; media, social pressure, fear-producing events, and the deception of false light teachings. At the same time, these lower frequency consciousnesses hijack the larger human collective which is already floundering about in the lower states of consciousnesses and is particularly susceptible to any programming that locks down the collective in control-matrices. These same Service-to-self entities, or consciousnesses which are disconnected from Source, also hijack Earth in a number of ways, using her energetic channels to transport trauma-generated energy to sustain their continued existence.

CHAPTER FOUR - BIOFIELD HIJACKING

According to the Cambridge dictionary, the definition of an entity is "something that exists apart from other things." Generally speaking, understanding of the word entity, whether benign or intentionally malignant, is that it is simply a consciousness that originates outside the self. An entity may be fully energetic, such as a spirit, or a dark overlord, or it can take on physical form, perhaps as an infestation of parasites and worms in the intestines and other internal organs. The goal of all entities is to survive and to feed, and the end result of human or animal connection to an entity is that nutrients, the life-giving force of the host, are being used to sustain the entity, which has no way to sustain itself. The most important thing to realize when considering what is meant by entities is a recognition that they exist on multi-dimensional levels and are both physical and energetic. Therefore, it is necessary to release them both from the physical, and from the energetic dimensions. The root source of the problem always begins in the energetic before it manifests in the dense, physical realm of the body. This is what is meant by the spiritual maxim "as within, as without".

Entities are not self-sustaining; they require a food source. This explains the concept of "loosh"; the trauma-based energy that parasitic consciousnesses feed from. In the last decade, a great deal of information about this subject has been shared from the perspectives of spiritually aware human beings across all walks of life. Bestselling author and holistic practitioner Dr. Christiane Northrup is an example; she discusses loosh and presents practical methods to deal with it in her book *Dodging Energy Vampires.* (Northrup. 2019). The terminology may be new, however, awareness that parasitic entities exist is not new at all. In the early 1900s, Rudolph Steiner categorized and detailed these consciousnesses extensively in his numerous books and lectures.

Human bodies retain energetic blockages in tissues and systems; these are frequencies that become trapped and held in place within the human biofield. Often, these blockages are quite accurately described as parasitic. They give off specific frequency signatures which match the frequencies of Earthbound spirits and other entities. At the end of the day, regardless of whether energy blockages come from consciousness and intention that originates outside of the self, or from a traumatic event that has been personally experienced and retained by the unconscious mind, the results are the same. With enough time, they can cause physical and psychological symptoms and progress towards serious manifestations of dis-ease. What began with a blocked emotion getting stuck somewhere in the body creates incoherence, and the frequencies it broadcasts are attractive to parasitic entities. They then look for ways to energetically attach themselves, so that they may receive benefits from the energy that is being either recycled, or causes a blockage in the surrounding energy that prevents it from flowing freely. Remaining in an unconscious, unhealed state places people at much greater risk than most are even aware of, which speaks to the importance of good spiritual hygiene.

The same principles are true for Earth. Trauma experienced by people and animals can become trapped in the Earth's biofield and held in place physically in the land itself. This attracts entities who feed on these frequencies. Blood sacrifice is an ancient, occult ritual that carries great power, and where life-giving blood is shed, the energetic signature is very concentrated and very strong. Biblical references to the power of the blood of Jesus Christ tell us that by simply speaking aloud the intention to invoke the protection found here, demons must flee. Different religious practices, both ancient and modern, arcane and traditional recognize the power of life that is represented by the blood.

Parasitic entities, human and otherwise, also install technologies that can harness this trapped energy and feed from it, creating a feedback loop that cycles continually to provide a never-ending food source for the feeder. Sometimes it is as simple as a ritual, repeated many times with the same intention. Once the traumatic event is healed and released, the cycle is finally broken, and often there is an energetic control mechanism in place that must also be sealed or removed.

Because of the magnitude of the suffering and the emotional charge that memories of holocausts, war, uprisings, and other catastrophic events have upon the collective, these traumas do not heal on their own. This is particularly the case when there is a physical implant technology deliberately holding the trauma locked into place upon the earth. Consider the September 11th Monument in New York and how it uses sacred geometry and occult symbolism to anchor the collective trauma of that terrible event in place. It also generates fresh loosh from the thousands of visitors who may not have had any personal connection to the events that happened there, but whose emotions become easily triggered when they visit the site. Black cubes represent a three-dimensional inversion of the Christian cross symbol; and two of these cubes have been embedded into the land itself, in a place where many survivors and family members now make ceremonial pilgrimages to. They remember and re-experience the horror, grief and the trauma that happened there in 2001. This implant technology is one of the most powerful and prolific sites of nourishment for dark consciousnesses that exists today on Earth, although there are many other such generators spread out across the planet. We find obelisk technologies and other monuments that commemorate bloody events placed strategically to siphon the trauma energy of the pain and the power of the spilled blood that is held locked into the Earth in these locations.

As people become aware of the purpose and the intentions behind the deliberate implantation of these technologies, they also become more conscious, and with consciousness comes the responsibility to act. This is one of the reasons why assisting the Earth to release the locked-in traumas to allow clearing and cleansing energies to once more flow is such an important goal for a gridworker. Because all life on the lands that surround these areas have been negatively impacted on a wide-scale, intentional work to release and heal the locations also has widespread beneficial effects.

Humanity itself has been hijacked in the same way that Earth has been hijacked. The personal energy vortices in the human body, the chakras, are the access portals into the multi-dimensional energy bodies of humans. Depending upon the implant technology and the individual's level of awareness (or lack of it), the potential harm that can be inflicted is often substantial, and it can affect every level from the physical body all the way up to the avatar. There are even some implants that are generational, causing entire families to suffer what are perceived to be inherited problems that can be physical, emotional, mental or spiritual. Generational traumas are carried within the cellular memory of every family member born into the family line, and they will remain there, energetically trapped until they can be released.

Emotion Code and Body Code are kinesthetic healing practices that can be used to identify the location and source of these types of blockages and to clear them. Deeply intuitive techniques; meditation, hypnosis, prayer, and quantum hypnosis, are other effective methods, and there are more and more new practices being brought forth in the gifts of many practitioners who are developing and evolving their own specialized methods. These practices and methods all fall under a growing umbrella of energy healing.

Some energetic implants are so powerful that they have negatively impacted entire tribes of people who all share the same DNA of origin. This is one of the ways that regressive entity consciousnesses have been able to control humanity for thousands of years by keeping us locked in cycles of misery and suffering. They also help to keep us in a state of amnesia; unable to remember our true history or to even recognize that incarnation here on Earth was never for the purpose of being debt slaves disconnected from each other and controlled by fear, forced to ask "the authorities" for permission to pay for the privilege of engaging in every single aspect of life. Another wonderful result of the rising levels of collective consciousness that has been referred to as The Great Awakening is that many people are becoming aware that what we thought was normal in the past is no longer acceptable. We are questioning why we ever thought it was acceptable in the first place! As we become more and more aware, we are also reaching for the tools that are available to assist us in raising our consciousness to greater heights.

Music is a particularly effective technology that can either heal or hijack. Many people are unaware (unconscious) of the fact that it even is a technology at all, or the way that it is used. Each chakra of the energy body has a consciousness all its own and carries a specific tonal frequency. When musical tones that correspond to the frequencies of the chakras are heard, the chakras open, which allows the music to enter the biofield where these organic frequencies set up a resonance that brings the entire system into balance and health. This is why music can have such a powerful and uplifting effect on consciousness. Many old churches still have the massive pipe organs that broadcast healing frequencies out into the surrounding areas; this is a very old technology that is infinitely more powerful than the new, artificially generated frequencies that digital technologies provide. A great many modern-day musicians have fallen into the same lower-density trap of trading the superior, infinitely-more-healthful organic frequencies produced by old, analog-based music for the convenience of artificial digital tones. Convenience has been the most insidious and effective of all long-term manipulations levied against the human population by dark consciousness loosh-eaters, and its siren song runs throughout the frequency fence that keeps us trapped.

Musical tones are also used to unlock the chakras to upload and install energetic implants and programming, and this explains why music has been used so deliberately for the purpose of subverting and controlling humanity. These techniques were admitted to have been utilized by governmental service agencies in the sixties as an integral part of the massive social engineering experiments that birthed the hippie peace movement of the time. The public was led to believe that this movement of peace, music and psychedelics was entirely organic, stemming from a generation who actively rejected the strict, authoritarian themes of their parents, however this belief could not have been further from the truth. By then, MK Ultra had already been running for nearly a decade; an entire system of mind control experimental programs deployed against the population by the CIA. Upon its discovery and the resulting public outcry, the government perpetrators pretended to terminate the program in 1973. This was another deception.

The lie was sold to a population who lacked discernment due to an overall low state of collective consciousness. The CIA simply moved their mind control programming plan underground. They did not shut it down as they led the public, and the Congress to believe. In the last few years, a great many survivors of horrific cult programming and ritual abuse have begun coming forward with their stories, seeking to reclaim their authentic voices and to find healing as they recover more and more of their memories. They all report that abuse and control has been ongoing for decades and is still very much a reality. (Worley, 2021).   The lengths that Service-to-self consciousnesses are willing to go in their endless quest to keep humanity trapped and prevented from ascension are endless, and that darkness is finally being brought into the light now so that it can be transmuted, and the lessons it was meant to teach fully integrated. This awakening of so many victims to the truth of what was done to them is yet another result of the increasingly higher states of consciousness that humanity and the Earth are now experiencing. In generations past, not only would these suffering people very likely be judged "crazy" by allopathy, but they would also simply be proscribed drugs to suppress their symptoms and have little chance to ever fully heal themselves. Now, these people find themselves part of a growing community of fellows who have also experienced the same violations of their free will, and there are many healers focusing on real solutions to help them that do not rely on ineffective methods that numb the pain and suppress the emotions while poisoning the body.

The recognition of the power of musical frequency and its profound effects on health and well-being go back thousands of years. The organic scale known by the ancients, and even referenced in Biblical texts was hijacked in 328 A.D. by the Roman Catholic Church and the Council of Nicea, which had gotten wise to the fact that church music had an uplifting effect on the consciousness of the peasants. This phenomenon was clearly a threat to the authorities, so knowledge of the ancient musical scales was conveniently "lost" along with certain Biblical texts and remained a closely guarded secret amongst the benefactors of the parasitic control systems which have been feeding upon humanity for hundreds of years. A new tonal scale based upon musical frequencies which are slightly incoherent and slightly out of sync with nature became standardized, and today this scale remains the standard of every first world country on Earth. The connections between the accepted musical standards and a number of high-profile, historically influential elite names are very telling and any serious music student should make a point of exploring history.

Discovery of the Dead Sea Scrolls, a vast cache of many of the hidden Books of the Bible in the 1940s was an energetic marker of the emerging Age of Disclosure. In the 1990s, naturopathic physician Joseph Puleo found the original divine musical code hidden in plain sight within the Book of Numbers in the Bible and identified the long-lost organic tonal frequencies that have since been dubbed the Solfeggio Scale.

(Mindvibrations, 2023). This hidden knowledge has slowly been infused back into collective awareness, and new healing modalities based upon sound frequencies are an integral part of the growing body of energy healing and alternative therapies. Because Earth herself emits energetic tonal frequencies, it stands to reason that music can be used deliberately to help her in her healing journey the same way that it can help humanity. Singing bowls, which began to appear in mainstream circles in the 1970s, are widely used during ceremonial gatherings, meditations and prayer circles, and their melodic voices balance the chakras. Percussion instruments such as drums and rattles have been used in spiritual practices by shamanic populations since time immemorial. These are all powerful tools that can also be used to assist Earth in much the same way that they assist the people of Earth.

CHAPTER FIVE: POLARIZATION

Life on three-dimensional Earth is an experience of polarities. Yin and yang, light and dark, good and evil; these are perceptual examples of energy dynamics that represent extremes. They are each a heads-and-tails component of what together make up an archetype. They are obvious and easy to recognize because they are extreme. Sometimes, the polarity of experiences and realities are not all that obvious, and a lesson for us here in this incarnation is to grow in our ability to recognize subtle differences. Polarity exists along a spectrum, and a great deal falls somewhere in the middle of the Bell curve; the mainstream, the zeitgeist, the normal. Humans have been programmed to view polarity through a lens of limitation; they categorize, and pathology is the goal. A tendency to compartmentalize and organize has been sold to us as necessary; a means to find safety and comfort in a mad, mad world. It is a hallmark of Scientism. It is also a limiting, close-minded view which is the opposite of expansion, and another example of polarity in and of itself.

Free Will can only exist where there is choice, and choice is taking deliberate action from inside the recognition of polarity. From a galactic perspective, the density of this planet and the way in which free will assists conscious manifestation is in and of itself the most challenging and rewarding of all soul missions, which is why incarnation on Earth in a physical, human body is considered such a desirable path for soul growth. The teachings of the Ra Collective, channeled through Carla Rueckert in the 1980s describe the choice to incarnate here into the experience that is Earth:

> The reason... is one that man on Earth has generated...out of desire. This illusion is useful. It is very useful for those who would wish to evolve at a very rapid rate by experiencing it and by using it while within it. Many of us now circling your planet desire to have the opportunity that you have...This is a way of

gaining progress spiritually and has been sought out by many of our brothers. (Ra, 1984, p 26).

From a higher dimensional level of consciousness where unity is the norm, where free will isn't necessary or even desired, and where manifestation is effortless, incarnation on Earth is the ultimate experience. The lessons to learn when you have suddenly disconnected from awareness of who you are, and the journey to remember and to re-learn what you have forgotten has a value that is beyond compare. The perspectives of The Law of One, as Ashayana Deane writes, teach that we are all part of an "interdependent universal brotherhood and co-creative evolution, practiced by advanced races who understand the interconnections between all life forms and reality systems" (Deane, 2002, p 36).

Although it has taken a long time for the average human consciousness, the "collective", to catch up, some core principles have long stood out as obvious, including a recognition of the sovereign right to walk the distinctive pathways of choice.

The Service-to-others path honors all life. It recognizes abundance and is where the original truth of Divine Source is found. If a teaching or a philosophy does not resonate with the essential principles of the Law of One, discernment allows the integrity (or lack) of the information to be felt so that the choice of action can be made. The Service-to-self path serves the ego-mind and is driven by a deep-seated fear of death, manifesting in control systems that exist on a belief in scarcity. Beings choose their own path, and this free will is what creates our "polarized universe, where all things exist within a duality of perception. It is this feature of (the) system that allows for the experience of free will to take place. Duality allows you the choice of breaking the rules or following, of working with the flow of natural evolution or against it." (Deane, 2002, p 123).

Duality is a key component to the experience of Earth incarnation because without contrast, clarity isn't possible. The problem for many is that they become stuck in misfortune, and the energy of lack becomes a blockage in their energy bodies. Rather than using the experience of what is not wanted as the springboard to manifest and create what is wanted, people become attached to the ego-identity of victimhood. This is a poignant lesson that has been shared by the human collective down through the ages, and the knowledge of it is certainly used by Service-to-self consciousnesses to trick humanity into manifesting situations which perpetuate their own enslavement. The victim and victimizer program is a soul trap that catches people very easily. Many remain stuck there, endlessly cycling back and forth between being disempowered victims of circumstances and being judgmental victimizers and are unable to see the cycle, much less break free from it.

Earth, a conscious being, exercises her free will by allowing herself to be the canvas upon which the different consciousnesses involved with and embodied inside humanity learn lessons within the framework of expressing or denying free will. She, too, is ascending now; and it is our actions and choices on her behalf that greatly assist in that process. Choices that assist her also assist us, as we and she are in a symbiosis with each other. Multi-dimensional awareness includes expanding into recognition of responsibility that extends well beyond the individual self.

Free will as it applies to Earth herself is not a subject that seems to be written about or widely acknowledged, however it is as relevant to her as it is to us. When undertaking gridwork, one should always have the intention of asking that the Earth be open to receive the benefits that are in full alignment with the spirit of that which the work is being done. This is simply a matter of coming from a place of humility with the intention to honor the rights of all beings to choose for themselves what they desire according to the Law of Free Will. Conscious awareness and full Presence in recognition of our shared Divinity with all beings is fundamental to spiritual practice in Service-to-others. This intention is part of the maintenance required of good spiritual hygiene. Free Will is a very important concept; in as much as one practices personal sovereignty, the process of freely allowing others the same rights as the self at all times ensures that one's own Free Will is consistently honored by others. As Above, So Below.

Interestingly, a large portion of the population is unaware that the mere act of participating passively in practices which violate other beings' Free Will is a mechanism of giving consent to allow their own Free Will to be violated. This is integral to the Law of Reciprocity. An example of this is oblivious (unconscious) participation in systems that are, at their source, inhumane and thus, anti-life. Consumption is the greatest of all unconscious mechanisms by which humanity participates and gives consent. In consuming meat that is factory-farmed and harvested in ways that cause suffering and pain for animals, people are giving their consent to allowing their own loosh energy to be harvested by parasitic entities. When we activate our Free Will and refuse to participate in supporting businesses that have these practices, we withdraw consent, and energetic balance can begin to be achieved. If it is not possible to abstain, either due to financial reasons or the lack of alternative food sources, the conscious act of giving thanks to the creatures who provided the meal and blessing the food helps to release the trauma and changes the entire energy pattern. This is the power of intention.

A large portion of the population is completely unconscious; applying tunnel vision to situations and preventing themselves from seeing the big picture and their own role in it. Another example of the Law of Reciprocity is the act of trampling upon the rights of others by allowing (or personally participating in) the use of social pressure to coerce others into behaviors that they do not choose. This gives consent to allow one's own rights to be free of pressure and influence to be violated in the same way. When we refuse to take responsibility for our own habits, bringing detriment to the well-being and health of others, animals and to the

Earth, we consent to allowing the same injury to ourselves. This reciprocity is what creates the energetic flow that enables the spread of microwave radiation technology such as 5G, and the increasingly tyrannical overreach of government service agencies, and the careless harm caused by industry in its never-ending greed for more and more consumption of its products. Ignorantia non excusat; ignorance of the law is no excuse and does not negate the consequences of trespassing. The same thing applies to the Cosmic Laws of the Universe.

Being unconscious is a choice, although it can be argued that due to the onslaught of deliberate, targeted poisoning that the world has been forced to endure over the last century, many humans do not have the physical capacity for discernment. The pineal gland is instrumental in determining the level of access that people have to their higher sensory perceptions, and environmental contamination in the air, water and soil has set the stage for pineal gland calcification. When the body is contaminated in this way, it can be as if the person was born without the organ entirely. This situation appears to stack the deck against our ability to give or withdraw consent consciously, and the simplest answer to that apparent contradiction lies with the soul contract of the individual and the choice of incarnation into this life facing these particular lessons. Many people experience a transformational awakening against all odds, and this speaks to Divine Timing and a plan that is being orchestrated at levels which go well beyond the boundaries of the physical world and our three-dimensional understanding of the forces at work in it. Miracles can and do happen every single day, and the power of prayer done for the benefit of others cannot be underestimated.

No conversation about polarity and Free Will can be complete without recognizing the evolutionary path of consciousness. From Source we come and to Source we return, and being at one with Source is Unity Consciousness. From that place, Free Will is not even a desired consideration, for the state of being at-one with Source is so encompassing that it is everything and there is no room for the desire to be separate. People who have experienced Divine Grace, and being in the Unified Field report that they did not want the feeling to ever end. Having felt that level of love and oneness, they did not want to have to return to their mundane "normal" lives and lose recognition of full connection with Source. Many people who tell stories of having had near death experiences, and those who have gone on high-level vision quests using Ayahuasca and other forms of ceremonial plant medicine share the same recurring theme. These people find themselves profoundly and forever altered by having gone through the experiences. This speaks to an entirely different level of consciousness than what is reflected in the priorities shared amongst the mainstream collective.

However, it makes sense that here on Earth, this would be the norm, if we are indeed here to learn soul lessons and attain growth through our experiences. There would be little motivation to create changes for the whole, without the contrast of struggle, suffering and questing…..and without the Free Will to choose our own different paths.

Now, we are being asked to consciously expand our perspectives beyond that which we have accepted as normal in the past, and to reach together toward the shared goal of unity consciousness, and Earth stewardship. This is a long reach, for certain. It is the complete antithesis of the messages that we took in growing up inside the hive of matrix programming. The covid era was a fast, an opportunity for us to completely reboot every part of our lives, both as individuals and as part of the collective. It was a time of transition, and now we are moving into transformation.

CHAPTER SIX: ENERGY FLOW

The three-dimensional perception of Earth, according to mainstream science is that of a spherical body in space, orbiting around a potentially harmful sun, with a physical core made of iron and nickel. This perception is a theory which has been taught as a fact in public schools and accepted by the mainstream for generations. It has never been proven. However, if you ask any scientist, intellectual, or even a high school biology student to describe Earth, this will likely be their answer. Interestingly, Geology that is taught in colleges is quick to claim this theory as fact, while at the same time denying the existence of ley lines.

The metal composition of the Earth's core emits frequencies which run through the layers of earth, dance across the surface and extend out into the atmosphere surrounding Earth. The sun generates a steady flow of electromagnetic energy to Earth, and it is absorbed and buffered by Earth's plasma magnetosphere, which disperses it. (Mckusick, 2021, p 91). Earth herself also generates her own electromagnetic energy, coined the Schumann Resonance, which was named in 1952 by professor and researcher Winfried Otto Schumann. "Schumann resonances are a set of frequencies of electromagnetic waves in the natural cavity formed by a planet's (moon's) surface and its ionosphere, in the extremely low frequency (ELF) range, caused by natural electrical activity of the planet (moon) and/or its atmospheric environment." (Bessler, 2007).

This vibratory hum, this "signature" of Earth, has been referenced since its discovery as a barometer of the collective consciousness of all life here on the planet. Its recognition, and the importance of its frequency is foundational for later discoveries in energetic frequencies that have formed the basis for many scientific disciplines, including Biofield-related Sciences. As Eileen Mckusick notes "the Schumann resonance......sometimes referred to as 'Earth's heartbeat'....is received by our pineal gland, which is composed of about 30 per cent magnetite, a type of iron oxide with natural magnetic properties," (Mckusick, 2021, p 97). The pineal gland is what has come to be recognized in the spiritual communities as the seat of the third eye; the chakra through which extrasensory (or beyond the limitations of the five physical senses) perception is enabled. Interestingly, this gland can also easily become calcified by drugs, fluoride and other toxic chemicals and metals which are coincidentally present in the "convenience" foods, products and treatments that have been sold to the populations of the Earth for many generations. Without active physical detoxing protocols, many people are physically prevented from having access to their own innate potential through the wisdom of their own bodies!

Rory Duff, a researcher from the United Kingdom, postulates in his work that the hum is the result of the frequencies coming from Earth's internal core, and physical evidence can be found in the electromagnetic and vibrational signatures coming through on the surface of the land in grid lines that can be detected by dowsing. Duff identifies several different categories of energy signatures, which translate into different expressions of lines, depending upon the frequencies. "Initially, the Earth Energies have been divided into those with an Electromagnetic nature, and those which are more likely to be ultra-low frequency vibrations.... further subdivided according to their widths, frequencies, nature and ultimate source." (Duff, 2023, p 31).

These energy signatures which originate from inside of the Earth herself, from the sun, and from galactic sources manifest into different types of lines on the Earth's surface. The energy lines always run in pairs, and each expand and contract, moving back and forth across the Earth to a specific degree over the course of hours or days, depending upon the strength of the energy signatures themselves.

Spherical, standing waves of sound, emanate like growing bubbles, from the center of the earth.

These waves bounce back, echo off, the changing rock type densities found both within the Earth's mantle and the Earth's crust and the Earth's surface. These rebounding sounds are what set up the standing waves and the two-way nature of these sounds. The stronger and weaker lines correspond to ...directions of standing waves with the stronger...coming straight from the center and the weaker...heading back to the center. (Duff, 2023, p 48-9).

The duality of these opposite-flowing currents is eerily like the traditional Indian concept of the Nadis which flow down and up the spine (or Shushumna, the central channel) of the human energy body; the Ida and the Pingala. The descending current is masculine and electric, and the ascending current is feminine and magnetic. Here is another example of how the biofields of all life here on the planet are patterned along the same template of our Earth. Leys and energy currents flow along Earth's surface in much the same way that energy currents flow along the body.

It is interesting to note that the most powerful of all frequency lines found on Earth, those of the lowest frequency which are termed Emperor Dragon lines, are believed to originate from galactic sources far away. These energy signatures, traveling great distances through space, were first detected decades ago, and at the time there were only three pairs crossing the entirety of the planet. Beginning in 2017, more pairs began to appear, and there is now a total of six known Dragon lines. Interestingly, the discovery in 2017 of a new Emperor dragon line running from pole to pole has been linked to several famous Indigenous prophecies including the Hopi End Times Prophecy. (Duff, 2023).

That these rare and special energetic signatures are coming online now, during this time, is a testament to how Earth is evolving. Dragons, much more than a creature of myth, hold great archetypal significance and represent power, royalty, strength and rejuvenation, among other things. They are one of the twelve symbols of the Chinese zodiac and play a very important role in Chinese culture. What could be the reason for this energy being strongly activated in the Earth's grid?

The places where energy lines of different strengths, frequencies and widths meet and cross over each other are called nodes. These are areas where Earth Energy is very concentrated. Frequently, these nodes result in geomantic structures; mountains, hills, and rock fixtures, and other symmetrical and asymmetrical shapes. Energy lines can be more electric, or more magnetic, and there are different strengths of the frequencies that these lines carry, which affect how they ebb and flow. Places where energy lines of the same frequency intersect are called large vortices, while the intersections of different energy lines are nodes. Rory Duff notes that North America has many large vortices; Sedona, Arizona is an example of a well-known area where this is particularly apparent, while upper Europe and the United Kingdom contain many more nodes.

(Duff, 2023, p 89). All these energies that run along the Earth's surface and below are known as Telluric currents. Sensitive people and animals can pick up on the energy emanating from these areas.

The expression of the Divine here on Earth that is Nature can be strongly felt along the pathways and byways running amongst the fields, the trees, the mountains, and the waters. Our ancestors did not obsessively follow a linear calendar in the way that today's materialistic societies have come to believe is normal, and instead marked the days by the seasons and in accordance with festivals that celebrated and honored different aspects of life. In times before our current technological age where people are so disconnected from Nature, there was a recognition that the Earth Spirit was omnipresent and omnipotent, and could be consciously felt; "like the energies of the human body, the spirit of the earth flows through the surface in channels or veins, and between the two energy currents of man and earth there exists a natural affinity." (Michell, 1973, p 12).

Sacred land sites where this energy concentrated naturally were identified and frequented by the people who gathered there to worship and have ceremony. Indigenous populations are still connected to this instinctive knowledge of Earth, aware of "a stream of magnetic current, fertilizing, and accompanied by manifestations of spirit, that passes through the country on certain routes and on certain days, its seasons determined by the positions of the heavenly bodies." (Michell, 1973, p 11).

These pathways, furrowed into the ground by many feet, marked the procession of indigenous people in celebration and worship, and were manifestations of intention through action. Journeying is action; just ask anyone who has ever gone on walkabout, or a vision quest, or a Shamanic Soul Retrieval Journey! The repeated enactments of intention embodied by their psychic or physical presence are what not only forged the line of the paths, but created the lattice of lines that mark the Earth's grid. These lines are known now as

Leys, named so by Alfred Watkins, a researcher of the 1920's.

Mainstream science continues to insist that this is "pseudoscience", however the ancient and practical reality of dowsing speaks a different truth, as does the last hundred and twenty years of research into plasma and quantum physics. Here is one more example of how the institution of science itself is designed to control and limit thinking, eliminating possibilities rather than expanding upon them. Rory Duff has spent many years charting leys in the United Kingdom, and he states that "people are just frightened of something new that might have a negative impact on hard-earned, pre-existing but possibly faulty, knowledge," (Duff, 2023, p 17).

It goes well beyond fear of being wrong; pushing against powerful forces that with deliberate intent have actively maneuvered and manipulated people into a rigidly controlled system that rewards conformity and destroys any threats to the existing control structures can be a dangerous proposition.

Dowsing is truly an example of how Earth Energy communicates, using the human body as a conduit. It establishes a barometer which marks through sensations the phenomena of the material world. This is very much the same way that the body expresses its inner knowing through the numerous now-recognized sciences such as Kinesiology, Emotion Code, and Biofield Tuning as described, respectively, by David Hawkins, Bradley Nelson and Eileen Mckusick. Indeed, this phenomenon is what explains how a pendulum taps into the body's inner recognition of truth and communicates answers to questions by swinging in a specific pattern.

Dowsing, the process of using a dowsing rod to find the presence of water beneath the ground, has been practiced effectively by intuitives for thousands of years. Long before the invention of electronic devices, this was the practical method that people used to find water and dig wells for their homes and their farms. Prior to the mid 1900s, dowsers were able to earn a decent living traveling around providing this valuable service to settlers. It has always been mainstream science of whatever current age that has attempted to discredit any effective techniques that are a threat to their financial interests.

Intuitive processes which tap into the energetic realms and empower humans to rely upon community and themselves have always been superior to man's artificial methods. The single true selling point for the artificial is convenience; therefore, that has been the underlying message which has driven society into a relentless addiction to instant gratification. According to Ken Roberts, the intuitive gifts of an accomplished dowser are far superior to the tools and techniques of the experts. "In the hands of competent dowsers whose Seventh Sense has been trained and sharpened, the rod points not only to water veins and domes over which the dowser is standing, but to water veins and domes at small and great distances from the dowser." (Roberts, 1953, p 6). Here, once again we reference the existence of senses that go beyond the limitations of the physical world that filters information through the limited score of the five obvious physical senses.

Dowsing with nothing more than a wooden branch and a finely tuned sensitivity was once a highly valued skill, in the days before the rise of our current social paradigm that demands formal schooling and layers of expensive certifications, all that was required were results. As Roberts notes in The Seventh Sense, "I cannot too often repeat that the rod of a skilled dowser will indicate EVERY spot along the course of a vein of underground water; never just ONE spot." (Roberts, 1953, p 115). The principal energy behind dowsing is communication between Earth and the human body, with the dowsing rod as the tool of measurement. Much of Rory Duff's work involves teaching people how to strengthen the innate sensitivity to this connection, and to trust it. Through the years, we have been taught not to trust our higher sensory perceptions, so there is a great deal to unlearn. Today, in 2023, the average person has never even heard the term dowsing; this is yet another testament to how far we, as a society, have moved away from our connection to Nature, and our trust in our own innate intelligence. It has been through the tireless work of people armed with little more than a hand-cut wooden dowsing rod that a very extensive mapping system of ley lines and energy lines across Europe and North America in particular, have been put to paper.

In View Over Atlantis, John Michell recounts how in the 1920s, researcher and scholar Alfred Watkins clairvoyantly saw a vision of England's Earth Energy blueprint one day.

> "The barrier of time melted and spread across the country, he saw a web of lines linking the holy places and sites of antiquity. Mounds, old stones, crosses and old crossroads, churches placed on pre-Christian sites, legendary trees, moats and holy wells stood in exact alignment that ran over beacon hills to cairns and mountain peaks." (Michell, 1975, p 15).

A merging of the divine archetypal energies occurs when science meets spirit, and each validates and confirms the other. A great deal of awareness comes to us intuitively through our third eye as clair-cognition, clairsentience and clairvoyance, and through our throat chakra as clairaudience. These are higher sensory perceptions; senses that exist outside of the five, finite physical body senses.

Michell reiterates how numerous locations across the countryside of England, Wales, Ireland and Scotland, recognized by the local populations as sacred sites, seem to fall along the same routes that follow linear paths across many miles in a way that is clearly not random. (Michell, 1975, p 17). Our ancestors, with their innate connection to the land, were very intuitive in feeling the Earth Energies, and their retracing the same pathways, tracks and roads that connected sacred sites of power also helped to further strengthen the energetic signature of the grid through their conscious awareness. These people were powerful gridworkers, knowingly or unknowingly; many of today's travelers who move about frequently, loving the feeling of an open road, are also gridworkers, and they are activating the paths that they journey along without even realizing what they are doing. In early 2022, the truck drivers who created long convoys across Canada and the United States to protest the governmental push of medical tyranny were activating North America's energy lines as they traveled with their powerful intentions. This is a beautiful example of a tribal gridwork mission, and the intentions and effects reverberated throughout the collective, raising the consciousness level of all life on the planet. Similar activities also happened across Europe, as people took united action to proclaim their rights to sovereignty.

Just as humans and Earth have similar energy channels; meridians, we both also have the same chakra blueprint. In 1967, author and mystic Robert Coons in communication with the prophet Elijah, is credited with bringing forth previously forgotten knowledge about the Earth's energy centers to the collective in his book *Earth*

Chakras: The Definitive Guide. "The study of Earth chakras is more akin to acupuncture in that we are exploring the more subtle energy structures of the Earth. Earth chakras are like bodily organs that are vital to the health of the world, and to all living beings dependent upon the various environments provided by the world." (Coons, 2009, p 3). Coons recognized the significance of energy vortices, connected by currents of energetic lines, and is credited with being one of the very first people to bring this information to print and share with the world. His seminal publication, and the earlier works of Rudolph Steiner detailing planetary correspondences together have informed a modern integrative collaboration between Robert Powell and David Bowden which resulted in their book, *Astrogeographia: Correspondences between the Stars and Earth Locations.* The work details the connection between Earth and Heaven and is a cosmic map of the Law of Correspondence. Seven primary Earth chakras can be found on seven continents which are connected by two primary Dragon Lines, and there are many, many other minor chakras which can be found connected to sacred sites across the globe. Powell and Bowden bring in recognition of the planetary correspondences in a discussion of how their qualities relate to the unique characteristics of these specific Earthly locations and their conclusions regarding the identification of each chakra differ from the chakra locations established by Coons, however his work served as great inspiration for their research. (Powell and Bowden, 2013, pp 1-12). In addition to being portals into Earth's energy bodies, Earth chakras are believed to be doorways, or entry points to locations in Inner Earth where ascended civilizations dwell. Down through the ages, there have been many stories of explorers who have found their way to legendary cities such as Agartha and Shamballa and returned with amazing tales.

It is significant to recognize that Earth's blueprint contains the same energetic pattern as the blueprint of the human body. The energies exist both within the physical body itself and extend outside of it. Just as the known currents of the physical human body, such as the flow of the bloodstream and the lymphatic system, the Telluric currents flow within Earth's physical body. And just as it is both the physical human body as well as the energetic currents surrounding us in the biofield together make up the human grid, all the energetic currents of the Earth's body and biosphere make up the Earth's grid. The inner composition of the Earth, with its aquifers, minerals, crystals and organic deposits; all with frequencies and consciousnesses, influence the shape and structure of the land around and above, and create energy patterns that can be felt and measured.

CHAPTER SEVEN: STAR GATES AND DNA

Star gates are important Earth architectures, all vastly powerful and all repositories of concentrated Earth Energies. Lack of current human understanding and even awareness of them does not negate their existence or their enormous potential; our ancestors were light years ahead of us in this comprehension.

Star gates are mighty interdimensional portals which exist slightly outside of our physical dimension, but whose energetic signatures resonate strongly in the physical bodies of anyone who is in proximity to them. (DeMarco, 2020; fssuniverse.org; gaia.com). These portals exist in the quantum field; they connect everywhere all at once and are not bounded by the physical laws of our three-dimensional Earth plane. Written accounts of the phenomena surrounding these portals continue to be dismissed by dogmatic mainstream science as coincidence and imagination, however the effects of interacting with these powerful locations are very real to the people who have experienced them, including contemporary researchers and authors such as Amanda DeMarco, Sandra Walters, Elena Danaan, and Dr. Michael Salla.

A star gate may be magnetic, electric, or a combination of both depending upon its environment and the signature of the elements in the lands which surround its three-dimensional location. Earth herself, in her current incarnation, has twelve interdimensional solar star gates which make up the twelve-sphere ascension template and connect on multiple levels to other galaxies and timelines. The number twelve is significant; it corresponds to the emanation of Creation and is an emanation of the 3-9-6 numerical pattern that is foundation to vortex math.

These star gates function like wormholes and have served as travel passages for galactic beings, both benevolent and malevolent, through the ages. A great deal has been written about this in the Keylontic Science teachings of the Voyagers series, Ashayana Deane's seminal work from the late 1990's. Each Earth star gate is keyed to a particular human DNA template pattern; tribes originally incarnated in specific geographic locations to serve as the guardians of that star gate, and it was only those who carried specific DNA coding who were able to open and access the star gates. Since the cataclysmic events that scrambled the angelic human DNA template and fragmented the higher strands, humanity has been living in a state of amnesia. The Service-to-self entities who have kept humanity enslaved for so long have also deliberately caused the further erosion of our DNA by poisoning our food, our water, our air and our soil. The degradation of our biological blueprint has moved us further and further away from our ability to activate the star gates, which is necessary for biological ascension. The same entities have also been heavily involved in genetic hybridization through the ages, gaining star gate access within their own racial lineages by genetically manipulating and combining the DNA of angelic humans with members of their own races. Control of the star gates has long been the goal of Service-to-self beings, who recognize Earth's unique place in the cosmos as a multi-dimensional, multi-universal access portal. Thanks to the amnesia created by the destruction and degradation of our DNA, humanity has been unaware of its great importance. We have treated it without reverence and have failed to secure and protect it at all costs. Commercial DNA tests have been eagerly bought by the public for the last decade merely to satisfy curiosity about one's ancestral lineage. People remain oblivious to the fact that they are voluntarily agreeing to allowing their own genetic harvesting.

The locations of star gates across Earth have been confirmed by numerous different spiritual teachers and experiencers, and most agree on the locations where the primary star gates can be found. Machu Picchu, Giza and Uluru house three very powerful, active star gates; visitors to these areas report feeling sensations of energetic charge registered by their physical bodies when they are within the vicinity, even though access to these portals is interdimensional. In addition to the twelve original solar star gates, there is a much younger network of Mother Arc star gates which were created for the purpose of the Indigo mission. These gates can be activated by the Service-to-other starborn races who have incarnated here on rescue missions in service to Earth and to all of humanity. (Ascensionglossary.com).

The composition and sacred geometric blueprint codes of each star gate is lesser known, and it is not as in depth of a focus for many, however this information can be obtained by tapping into the higher perceptory senses. By focusing all attention on a particular star gate in meditation with the intention to communicate with the gate and to receive information, one can end up with a completely different perception than what someone else might receive. We all come to a place of understanding through the unique filters of our own cellular memory of genetic lineage and galactic history, as well the limitations imposed by our current levels of consciousness. Any shadows, any wounds, any unhealed traumas and lessons that we have not yet addressed in this lifetime play a part in the filters through which we receive and process information. Additionally, memories of past lives and family histories that are intact and contained within our energetic DNA color the lens through which we view information. History is very different when it is told from the perspectives of those who experienced life following different religions and belonging to different races and social classes. Personal experience and the experiences of close family members exert very strong influences that color our individual and collective histories and affect how we receive information. The world really has very few examples of humans who are truly free of any kind of bias at all. Generally, only those rare individuals who have reached such a high level of consciousness that they are able to view everything from a place of unity and acceptance are able to maintain pure objectivity.

Inner knowing and the ability to be sensitive and receptive to information has much to do with the condition of our physical bodies. Our physical vessels are directly tied to our biological ascension and our ability to reach higher levels of consciousness. Many spiritual teachers fail to give this truth the attention that it truly deserves. Spirituality is holistic, yet this recognition has not yet been fully actualized in the collective consciousness.

Detoxification and repair of our physical template is part of the important work that humanity must focus on. It is not enough to meditate and devote all attention to inner work, healing past traumas and prior life wounding. Consciousness here on the three-dimensional Earth plane goes hand in hand with biology. Our bodies are the actual vehicles of ascension, and consciousness is not separate and distinct, but interconnected. This interconnectivity has been demonstrated many times over and is a well-recognized phenomenon, even within mainstream circles. The physical process of focused breathwork, for example, activates biological processes that release a flood of plasma into the pineal gland and allow us to connect with Source consciousness. Anyone who has ever used plant medicine can testify to the spirit-mind-body connection that takes on instant clarity during a journey. Yoga can produce many of the same effects, as can Chi Gong, and numerous other disciplines that are grounded in physical, spiritual practices. Diet also has a very powerful effect on consciousness; it can cause the body to retain density or to release it, and it can either hinder spiritual growth or accelerate it. It is no coincidence that the Bible has many examples of how fasting was used by the ancients as a method of connecting with God; this practice not only contributes to physical health and longevity and greater vitality, it also lifts consciousness by allowing density to fall away. The mind-body connection is very real and is often underappreciated by our instant-gratification society, and any so-called spiritual gurus who skip over this fundamental truth should be viewed with skepticism. This is an example of spiritual bypassing.

Grounding is a very important practice of connecting to Earth, and it allows the organic currents and support from our Divine Mother to flow through our bodies and balance us in ways that can have an almost magical effect on health. Bare-footed connection to the land discharges the build-up of electromagnetic frequencies that disrupt our biorhythms and cause stress, which has a great deal of cumulative negative effects on health. It has been known to even dispel the symptoms of Herxhelmer; which is a term describing a variety of uncomfortable physical symptoms that result from the purge of toxins from the body and have the appearance of allergic reactions. Interestingly, in the 1970s, the introduction of synthetic rubber and man-made shoe soles marked the beginning of a period when humanity began to collectively experience rampant inflammatory problems in the body that had never been seen before. A whole host of inflammation-related maladies began cropping up; an underlying contributor of dis-ease that was nonexistent before that time. Of course, the actual root cause of this condition remains a mystery to mainstream allopathic medicine, which could not connect dots even if there was funding provided for it to do so. It is very important that there be an actual connection to a healthy, uncontaminated Earth. Attempting to put bare feet down onto an asphalt parking lot will not allow for the free flow of energy up from the Earth into the body.

The same regressive-consciousness beings who have enslaved humanity and inverted all systems for thousands of years have worked diligently to ensure that we remain disconnected from Source, the Earth, and our own cellular memory of who and what we truly are. As the consciousness levels have been rising in the 20th century, their deliberate hijacking has ramped up in an attempt to counter it. Not only have massive amounts of chemical toxins been pumped into the environment through geoengineering (also known as cloud seeding) since the 1940s, but pharmaceutical poisons have increased exponentially and are now keeping much of the population dependent, and in a state of constant fear over dis-ease. I do not say fear over health, because a focus on true health removes fear, and puts the power back into the hands of the individual, where it belongs. Detoxification and parasite-elimination are not even touched upon by allopathic practitioners, yet they are fundamental to holistic health of the body. These concepts are also important for the health of Earth, and as we move forward with the deliberate intention of creating the world that we want to live in and to leave to our children, it will become more and more important for humans to take an active role in figuring out how to assist Earth with detoxing and removing parasite infestations from the land and the environment. It is also necessary for humanity to step forward and put a stop to the ongoing and deliberate pollution that has been occurring throughout the last century. For that to happen, though, it is first necessary for humanity to acknowledge that it actually is happening, and to reclaim their lost power.

We are fortunate that the times we are living through now are beginning to allow us the opportunity to once more know the ancient truths that humanity once took for granted. Source, and the cosmos are working together, assisting us to break free from the chains of slavery that we were unaware were binding us. The incoming light codes from the sun, and the photon belt activations that are bombarding Earth are helping to restore the original DNA patterns, which is triggering cellular memories and slowly bringing people back online. It truly is an exciting time to be alive on Earth.

CHAPTER EIGHT: CRYSTAL ARCHITECTURES

Where Earth Energy is concerned, the power and importance of crystals cannot be understated. More than just pretty rocks that are harvested from deposits under the ground, they have consciousness all their own, and every crystal has its own unique frequency. These are beings who thrive and grow with life force energy. A crystal that is traumatized loses its potency and can even die. It is not a random thing that Earth's voluminous underground caverns are vast repositories of naturally forming crystals; these are a structural part of Earth's architecture, and they contribute to the multi-dimensional consciousness that makes up her energy body. Their energies pour into the energetic currents that run along Earth's grid and pull energy back from them in a gigantic feedback loop that has discernible effects on the landscape surrounding the deposits.

Beneath the mountains around Little Rock, Arkansas lies the largest unbroken vein of quartz crystal in the world, spanning many miles and pulling nourishing energy from the ley line-generated vortex of this region. Hidden here, deep underground, are the crystals that powered the ancient civilization of Atlantis. They were spirited away to protect them just before the cataclysm destroyed the majority of Atlantis' landmass. The depth and significance of this massive crystal repository is not even on the radar of most people going about their matrix lives, but the time will come when humanity becomes aware of how much of our true history has been hidden.

Similarly, there are other locations around the world that have been rediscovered in the last several decades and generate amazement and curiosity. One example of a discovery that did receive media attention occurred in 2013, when miners digging near Chihuahua, Mexico were astounded to find a cave filled with selenite crystals. These structures are so massive, the discovery so unexpected, that it garnered quite a bit of media attention. Whenever these rediscoveries are made, there is always a sense of wonder and awe, but little mainstream awareness of the vast potential that these vessels of consciousness contain, and exactly how powerful they are. Lemurian seed crystals are another example of how crystals are a powerful repository of consciousness. They are found in Brazil, in a location where ancient Lemuria was said to have existed, and each crystal contains "memories" which are believed to be able to help humanity to access soul memories connected to this lost civilization where the collective consciousness was very high. Herkimer diamonds, a type of quartz crystal that can only be found in the mines located in upstate New York in the town of Herkimer, are another example of a unique crystal. These quartzes can amplify energies in a very powerful way, and their consciousness levels emit very high frequencies.

Star forts are man-made crystalline architecture built to channel the vortex energies that exist where land and water converge. History proclaims artist Michaelangelo as the designer of the first known star fort, built in the sixteenth century to shelter the Medici family from attack; there are now hundreds of star forts in existence all over the world, created in the same star pattern, and these structures remain places of immense Earth Power. (Stuemke, 2023). Star forts are an example of how crystal technology is used with intention to channel and direct energy for a specific purpose. Chad Stuemke, a researcher, author and speaker from Michigan has written a great deal from his research surrounding Detroit and its Star Fort and other sacred sites, which tap into the Earth Energies recognized by the Indigenous Tribes who came before the European settlers.

The 42nd parallel has a strong connection to Native American tribal wisdom and power, and old ley maps can sometimes be located which detail a thick line that extends across the Northeast part of America. Recall that the Nations making up the Iroquois Confederacy were from this region, and their society was a shining example of equality, respect for the land and for the guiding wisdom of the elders and the Divine Feminine in action. Benjamin Franklin was reported to have spent several years living among the Iroquois, and he brought forth many principles that he learned from their advanced society with the intention that they be incorporated in the Founding Documents of America. Although the distorted consciousness of patriarchal mentality that was embedded in the zeitgeist of the time overshadowed much of his attempts, he was able to insert some elements and intention into the Declaration of Independence, and the spirit of equality from these very high-consciousness documents continue to resonate to this day. Kinesiology measures the consciousness of the Declaration of Independence to be between 700 and 1000; it is an incredibly high-level and ascended document. (Hawkins, 1995).

Galactic history as communicated to contactees through dreams, visitations, channeled messages, and Clair senses, connects the dots and many practitioners have discovered the amazing power of crystals through working with them. The Ascension Glossary states, "In planetary history, **Crystal Caverns** were used as internal power crystal generators and for data memory storage for the planetary brain. Ultimately, these clusters are remnants of what is left of crystals that were misused in the Atlantean time cycle. They were exploded underground and created a large cataclysm on the surface." (Renee, 2013). The deliberate manipulation of these powerful consciousnesses by human and non-humans alike can have very significant consequences.

Crystals can be used as tools, and their use depends upon the intention of the user. These truths remain unexplored and unknown by the sleeping masses. The stone monoliths of Stonehenge, made from a rare form of quartz, are an example of how this technology continues to baffle contemporary minds which limit themselves in the worship of scientism. Stonehenge is one of most obvious and well-known instances of crystal technology placed with intentional purpose in a geographic area that resonates with strong Earth Energy.

There are many vast deposits of crystals located beneath the earth which are undisturbed; repositories of raw power and conduits for specific intentions broadcast out to earth through the channel of her energetic lines. These crystals contain the potential for enormous changes to the surface of Earth and have been used by advanced civilizations of the past.

One of the most intuitive of psychics in more recent history, Edgar Cayce, known as "the sleeping prophet," for his powerful and accurate messages channeled while he was in a trance, spoke many times of the lost civilization of Atlantis and its powerful crystal technology. Cayce's work confirmed much of the writings of earlier philosophers Plato and Francis Bacon. (Childress & Clenendon, 2000, p 239). The information that Cayce brought forth captured the imaginations of many questing souls who resonated with the ideas. "The terrible crystals of Atlantis; the subject of Atlantis and the Power System of the Gods, starts with the knowledge of Tesla's wireless transmission of power and then moves on to more subtle information, that of psychic sources". (Childress & Clenendon, 2000, p 229). Many stories tell that it was the misuse of these crystals that caused the destruction of the technologically advanced Atlantean civilization, who had themselves moved away from practicing Service-to-others, and instead were dedicated to power and prioritized control over a respect for Earth and for all life.

Crystals are very important tools, as they have naturally formed consciousnesses all their own which vibrate at specific, measurable frequencies, and they grow and develop in many different compositions and placements in caverns and other underground locations. Their ability to store and discharge energy, as well as to retain the specific frequencies that they embody in a pure and unchanging form, have been well-known since time immortal. They are instrumental components in the manufacturing of many of the technologies that mainstream science-directed societies depend on to function and thrive, including transistors, computers, vehicular components, and many others. They were utilized by ancient, highly advanced civilizations for power, locomotion, healing, and energy delivery.

Well beyond Stonehenge, many of the ancient technologies remain visible today, although the full extent of what these technologies are capable of has been largely forgotten. The lands of England, Scotland, Ireland and Wales have other similar monolithic structures dotting the countryside and many of them predate Stonehenge. The Calanais Stones, which have stood on the Isle of Lewis in Scotland for over 5000 years and the Ring of Brodgar are two such examples. It should be noted that the monoliths of these stone circles do not have capstones, like Stonehenge. Crystals are tools, and their shapes and placements allow energies to be directed in a specific way. Capstones speak to different intentions behind the original placement of these giant structures than is evident in other stone circles across the planet.

Another example of crystal technologies which hide in plain sight are the stone obelisks that can be found in epicenters of activity in militaristic societies. There are many theories and stories written about the purpose of these structures, the majority of which are made of solid crystal. Cleopatra's Needles, Washington Monument, and the Bunker Hill Monument are all examples of these structured technologies, and various researchers of more esoteric knowledge and a greater recognition of the intentional use of symbolism in the material world have presented different explanations through the years. These explanations postulate the purposes for these structures as ranging from pure symbolism designed to flaunt an authoritarian mindlock of government control systems (as according to the late Jordan Maxwell), to monuments created to honor the epic egos of dead monarchs and rulers, to working components of ancient astronomical observatories. David Childress observes, when describing the proximity of obelisks to ancient, sacred Egyptian buildings, "These strange 'solar temples' with their obelisks and causeways look a lot like a ceremonial imitation of an actual power station." (Childress & McClendenon, 2000, p 267). His ideas about the active nature of these technologies are close to the mark, considering the nature of the crystals themselves.

The shape of these structures is strikingly like that of a cut crystal wand, with the same proportions that include a wide-based, magnetic female side and a narrow, electric masculine side. This is no coincidence. Crystal wands are tools of focused intention, and it is therefore easy to recognize that these shapes are not merely monuments but are conduits to actively transmit Earth energy. While a reasonable question to ask might very well be to "where, and on whose behalf?", what is more important than the answer to that question is the recognition of the real effect that these structures have on the body of Earth, and on the surrounding life. By looking at the effects, one can discern the original intention. As we have previously observed; all consciousness has an energetic signature, and the energy of emotion is powerful. When trauma becomes locked into the land much the same way that it becomes locked into the body, blockages occur that stop the natural flow of health. Additionally, the esoteric shape of the structure itself can serve as a conduit to harvest and siphon energy from an original event indefinitely, to feed lower states of consciousness. Capstones divert the flow of energy and recirculate it back down. The placement of these crystals speaks to deliberate intention of the architects.

There are many ways that Earth's Energies can be intentionally strengthened to heal the land, to harness and siphon it, to suppress and mute it, and even to channel it in a way that causes deliberate harm and destruction. An example of a non-crystal technology that can be used in a way that is either beneficial or detrimental depending upon the intention of the user are Crop circles (Deane, 2002, p 187-188), which are a way that galactic beings "code' the land with frequencies, transmitted with the use of sacred geometry. Language is very powerful, and symbolism is the most advanced of all known languages, and the highest of which humanity is capable. These patterns transmit symbolic messages to the land, and to the subconscious minds of all the beings who experience them and are able to activate humanity and Earth energies. In the 1960's, researcher Gerald Hawkins delved into the connection between the geometric patterns of crop circles and sound frequency, and since his time, many others have confirmed and added to a growing body of knowledge surrounding these technologies. (Gaia, 2019). The United Kingdom continues to host approximately thirty new crop circles each year, and this location is by far the most prolific receiver of these messages. As this area also has the heaviest concentration of ley line intersections known in the world, it is a potent sign for those with eyes that see and ears that hear. It is not a coincidence that so many monuments that pique curiosity and imagination are prevalent all across these ancient lands, where many

legends and myths have been woven into the cultural
fabric of the people who live there.

CHAPTER NINE: WORKING WITH THE GRID

Grid working, a relatively new term for any activity that involves the intention of supporting, helping to heal, or catalyzing positive change to the Earth's physical and/or energetic grid template, is taking responsible action. It is our sacred human duty, as stewards of the Earth. Gridworking is work done in the physical; out in nature, involving ritual, anchoring through the planting crystals or other tools, going on pilgrimages, making offerings, and essentially anything else done out in the three-dimensional world that is intentional. Gridworking is done when a lightworker travels and consciously projects healing out across the land. It is done through energetic intention; meditation, prayer, group ritual, energy techniques that employ remote viewing. It is also done in the physical world through quantum entrainment: by setting up a crystal grid in one's personal space with the intention that its energies work to clear and heal a distant place.

the site, the effects are greatly amplified with the addition of tools and anchors. Crystals are used to both charge and to amplify, and they are an extremely effective addition to any grid working project; whether done remotely or in the physical world.

People who find themselves drawn to actively practice this work receive great benefits by becoming familiar with the many different types of crystals and their correspondences. Taking a class, reading a few books or even researching on the internet is an excellent starting point. Crystals are of the Earth herself, they are grown in and nourished by Earth Energy, and this in turn allows them to magnify and radiate these energies out across the land. At the same time, they send nourishment back into the Earth in a continuous, sustainable loop. They are very important in gridwork. Their frequencies, like the DNA of humans, are tuned to the specific areas where they are found, and these energies can be directed intentionally.

Although all life on Earth is primarily carbon-based, the container that is silicon-based can hold higher states of consciousness consistently due to its geometric structure, which corresponds to specific frequencies, depending upon the type of crystal. The Piezoelectricity that emanates from crystals is stable and enduring, unlike the changing energy patterns that ebb and flow with unawakened humanity's emission of emotions. Humans are largely unconscious, and this is partly due to the lack of awareness, and a focus on survival. Our creative powers are always at work, but when we remain unconscious of this truth, we allow ourselves to be used. Our emotions, the magnetic energy, which is half of the creation equation, can be manipulated, steered and used by outside forces to further *their* aims and agendas.

Media is the primary mechanism that Service-to-self consciousnesses use to keep humanity under perpetual hypnosis; its role is to generate certain emotions upon command through some program, amplify the emotional charge, and direct it toward specific manifestations that benefit the controllers. The way that the entire phenomenon known as "predictive programming" is currently understood is inverted. Desired outcomes are presented in movies and stories to foment emotion, so that humanity can do the creative work to manifest these outcomes. While Free Will does require voluntary consent, and Service-to-self entities utilize the principle of *revelation of the method* to obtain unwitting consent by all who fail to object to it and consent by default; they would not be able to execute any plans without human manifestation.

Service-to-self consciousness is disconnected from Source. Therefore, it is incapable of creation, only of mimicry. This is why humanity is constantly being manipulated into creating outcomes through coercion and deception. If every single person who watched an Armageddon-event movie were to internally flip the script and visualize a different positive outcome for the world rather than falling into shock, fear and a feeling of powerlessness, the dark, negative agendas would fall away quickly.

This is the single greatest truth wherein lies the potential for us to reclaim our sovereign power; and recognition of this is essential for our evolution into consistently higher states of consciousness as a species. The "learn to discern!" drumbeat has been reverberating throughout the spiritual community for many years now, and the message is becoming more and more urgent.

Interestingly, bones, cartilage and teeth are crystal-based infrastructure in the bodies of humans and animals, and the bone marrow is where new cells are continually created. Again, we share our biological structure with that of Earth. As humanity evolves into higher states of consciousness, so, too, does our biology evolve into a more crystalline energetic structure, and this in turn increases our ability to work harmoniously with crystals.

Now is a time in history where it becomes increasingly more important for gridworkers to step forward and activate their sacred missions. The Earth's grid has been under siege for eons, and as consciousness rises on the planet, so do the efforts of Service-to-self consciousnesses to squeeze all of humanity. Wormholes and inorganic vortices, implants that steal energy and block flow, recycling technologies, electromagnetic technologies and control-tower technologies are just a few examples of deliberate tampering with the Earth's grid. The natural current of energy signatures can be reversed, changed, magnified, blocked and what is organic and life giving can be manipulated so that it becomes life siphoning. The effects of these intentions are all expressed in the evidence of the surrounding lands and the people who live there. While more and more people are able to recognize the connection between country living and overall health as it contrasts to city living, we generally attribute much of these effects to socio-political reasons. This is only the most visible and surface level of awareness.

A great deal of our understanding of the world has been very superficial. We must get deep below the surface, expand our awareness into the caverns and aquifers, into the veins and the channels below. We must consider the electric and the magnetic signatures and recognize that this is an expression of the Law of Gender here on the material plane. We must study and integrate fully the cosmic, universal laws, the principles which undergird every aspect of the world that we live in. In doing so, we begin to recognize where these universal laws are being manipulated and distorted. We must expand our awareness of Tesla's teachings that everything in the Universe is energy and vibration and apply that awareness to our planet. All life on Earth is affected by Earth energy.

CHAPTER TEN: CRYSTAL TOOLS

Crystals host specific frequencies, evidenced by their molecular structure, colors and properties, and each and every crystal is tuned to the frequency of a particular chakra. This is true whether it is a chakra in the human energy body, or a chakra that is connected to the energy body of Earth. A great deal of knowledge has been gathered over the course of many years (even through mainstream scientific studies) and the power and potential of crystals is much more well-known to the powers-that-be than the public even imagines.

Marcel Vogel, a brilliant researcher, chemist and inventor from the mid-1900s, is well-known for his many patents and extensive work with quartz crystals. After he retired from a long, distinguished career as a non-degreed scientist at IBM, he went on to found his own laboratory, Psychic Research, Inc, to dedicate himself full time to researching energy signatures of the body; what has come to be referred to as the biofield.

Through his work, Vogel realized the power of love to be a consciousness with a specific frequency, something which set him light years ahead of the scientific zeitgeist of the time.

Very early on in his research, he recognized the energy storage ability of crystals and instinctively knew that in order to harness their power, a method to direct it was needed. He worked tirelessly to develop a technique to channel and focus the energies to create a beneficial effect in the three-dimensional world. Old videos of his teachings and live crystal healings for many people can be found just by searching the internet, and his work continues to inspire the younger generations every day. Marcel Vogel eventually was able to devise a method of cutting the facets of quartz crystals with very specific geometric precision; it is said that this blueprint came to him clair-cognitively from Pleiadian intelligence.

At the time of this writing, the number of individuals still alive today who were personally trained by Marcel Vogel to cut crystals using his procedure can be counted on one hand. According to the Marcel Vogel Legacy group, a foundation dedicated to preserving his immense contributions as a bridge-builder between science and spirit, the human body as crystalline is based in solid, scientific research.

> The crystal is a quantum converter that transmits energy in a form that has discreet biological effects. The human body, on an energetic level, is an array of oscillating points that are layered and have a definite symmetry and structure. This crystallinity is apparent on both a subtle energetic or quantum level as well as the macro level. The bones, tissues, cells, and fluids of the body have a definite crystallinity about them. (Their) structure… tends to become unstructured or incoherent when dis-ease or distress is present... Through the use of an appropriately tuned crystal to which these structures are responsive, balance and coherence can be restored by delivering the

necessary "information" or energetic nutrients needed. (marcelvogellegacy.com).

If we apply that same focused intention to improve areas of our lives, and to heal Earth that we apply to healing the body using crystals, we will find that we get the same results. Crystal energy healing has been practiced effectively outside of the mainstream for many years and has had significant results for animals and people.

Many practitioners utilize crystals to create grid patterns with the intention of manifesting different outcomes for personal success, luck, health, happiness, and love; there are websites and books in print that give guidance to people interested in doing this work. These crystal grid patterns can be used as the focal point of a process that involves creating a space and directing intention to manifest a beneficial, desired outcome from a quantum perspective. The grid pattern is laid out in a safe location where it will not be disturbed, and quantum entrainment is the energetic process that assists the manifestation of the outcome.

All crystal grids, regardless of whether they are planted outside in the land or set up in an undisturbed location in a house, are tools for intentional, directed manifestation. They can all be set up using the same simple, fundamental components; a geometric pattern, carefully selected crystals, and an intention. Central to the grid is the centering guidestone, with crystals that represent the concentrated energies of the intended result, crystals to magnify and radiate the intentions within the pattern itself, and crystal points for the outside. Depending upon the practitioner, there may also be other additional tools to help bring clarity and energy to the grid itself, such as a map of a particular location that is being targeted, or special, personal items that hold the energy of the intentions.

The first step is for the grid worker to clarify exactly what it is that she wants to achieve, and for whom. Is it to manifest something specific in her life, or on behalf of her family? Is it to release trauma that is locked in the land, and heal not only the Earth but also the surrounding communities and the wildlife there? Getting clear on the scope of the work, and the desired outcome is a very important part of any type of healing, and it is often surprisingly difficult for people to identify. Often, people are much more focused on what they do not want, rather than homing in on what they do want. While finding clarity through contrast is a very effective method to answer this question, people sometimes do not use the comparison in an intentional way and end up stuck in a loop where they concentrate all their attention and energies manifesting the things that they do not want.

The process can be as simple or as complicated as feels right to the gridworker. Take whatever time is necessary to figure out exactly what it is that you do want before you do anything else. This is an important part of intention and goes well beyond grid working.

After clarifying the goal, the next step is to find symbols that hold the same energetic frequency of the outcome that you desire. This helps you decide which crystals should be used in the grid. One way to explore this question is to consider the chakras and figure out which of them are tuned in to the goal that you have in mind. If, for example, you are seeking to step out of fear and into your personal power by launching a business or taking a bold move to do something new that you've always wanted, activating the electric, masculine will-power of the solar plexus chakra will help bring the changes that you need. Citrine, pyrite, amber and golden topaz are all crystals that are tuned to the frequency of the solar plexus chakra; all are found in different shades of yellow, gold and brown, and any of these crystals would be an excellent addition to this crystal grid. With the internet, learning about crystal correspondences is very easy, and the information is plentiful.

You will want to select some crystals that are amplifiers of energy, such as quartz, to help empower, direct and radiate the intention of the grid outward. Also select additional crystals whose frequencies are supportive of your goal, such as tiger eye, which is tuned to all three of the lower chakras, particularly to the root chakra. It represents grounding, protection, security and stability. Crystals that represent Source frequency, such as selenite, keyed to the crown chakra, add their power to the grid. I tend to use selenite crystal as the central stone for many of my crystal grids, regardless of specific intention for the outcome. This is because the crown chakra is the point at which Source energy comes in through the physical body, so it feels right to me. Do what you feel called to do. You can use many crystals, or few; it all depends on your preference.

The number of crystals that you will be using will have a lot to do with the geometric pattern that you have chosen. Sacred geometry is an important part of ascension mechanics and should be studied to achieve a level of understanding of the different patterns and what they symbolize. Base 12 geometry reflects the pattern of original Source Creation; twelve is the number of perfection and completion, and mathematically expresses the 2:1 natural order of the Universe. In the early 1900s, William James Sidis, a theoretical physicist and child prodigy published his seminal work *The Animate and the Inanimate,* which explored dark matter, black holes and established a twentieth century foundation of understanding of the significance of Base 12 geometry to Creation. In 1936, his contemporary, German physicist Burkhard Heim expanded awareness of the Base 12 coding into the twelve dimensions of Quantum Theory. However, much of the sacred geometry that is well-known today is Base 10 and incomplete.

Many spiritual teachers believe that the same Service-to-self consciousnesses that have created inversions within every organic system also use inverted sacred geometry to hijack energies and reduce the effectiveness of well-intentioned activities. The Metatron's Cube is one familiar example of this; it is believed that this pattern is a Saturnian hijacking and suppression of the Sacred Feminine principle. Another example is the daisy of death versus the flower of life; both patterns contain geometry in different angles, and it has been argued that the mathematical formulas that derive from these patterns can be proven to either continue to self-sustain by perpetually expanding, or to eventually subtract themselves out of existence. I recommend that people explore the subject in some depth, then decide for themselves which patterns resonate with them.

After my very first simple grid, I began using the Flower of Eternal Life pattern extensively, and this particular shape allows for numerous crystals to be placed on the many points where the lines of the pattern cross. Now that I have done many grids, I have moved into less complicated patterns which allow me to pare down the total number of crystals to give better focus to my specific intentions. Gridworking is a personal evolution, and as you do, you learn, and your work becomes more instinctive.

Many people begin their gridworking practice by creating a crystal grid in their homes, focusing on a personal intention, rather than by going outside and burying crystals in the ground in a more permanent way. This method has been popularized by numerous modern crystal healing practitioners. A simple internet search can turn up a great deal of guidance and many examples. There are also hard-copy books that have been written by grid workers who have employed these practices to help people create positive changes in their lives. One such practitioner, Kiera Fogg, has used crystals for many years, and her working knowledge of the properties and strengths of different crystals is very helpful for a novice who is learning the basics. She states in her book, *Crystal Gridwork: The Power of Crystals and Sacred Geometry to Heal, Protect and Inspire* "setting your intention is by far the most critical step in building your crystal grid. It is only by way of setting compelling, spiritually aligned intentions that our grids can hold any real power at all." (Fogg, 2018, p 14). This book is just one concrete source of information for a fledgling gridworker; there are many other authors and practitioners who bring forward other useful pieces of the puzzle.

Energymuse.com is another website that provides guidance and many good visuals to help people learn about crystal grids and sacred geometry. There are also numerous courses about crystal correspondences and crystal healing that can be accessed from a variety of popular educational platforms such as Udemy, MindValley, and Teachable, as well as directly from numerous dedicated practitioner websites and YouTube channels. One thing should be noted; students must not make the mistake of dismissing sources that have been around for decades (or longer) as obsolete. Many powerful teachers have brought highly relevant information forward in the past, but they have frequently fallen into obscurity because these people were light years ahead of their time. The writings of Rudolph Steiner, born in 1861, continue to inform the work of a great many modern-day students of esoteric disciplines. With over three hundred fifty lectures and published books, he was a true galactic historian and a spiritual alchemist, and his ideas are woven throughout many disciplines as we know them today, establishing him as one of the most widely influential thinkers of our current era. Organic agriculture and alternative, child-centered education are two areas which are very powerfully informed by his original work. Never forget that what eventually becomes "mainstream" was once on the fringe. Even in the scope of this work, it is interesting how many discoveries began in the 1970s and earlier (at this writing, more than fifty years ago!) that are being widely utilized now, and merge different disciplines.

The current digital age makes information much more readily accessible than it once was and provides a doorway in the current age for us to easily step through, while fundamental knowledge of great value was once actively being suppressed. A well-rounded individual seeks always to expand consciousness through multiple access points, and many of the older sources of knowledge provide a solid foundation upon which more contemporary, readily accessible information has been built.

CHAPTER ELEVEN: GRIDWORK ON THE LAND

It is extremely useful to integrate fundamental knowledge of the different structures of crystals and their embodied frequencies to begin targeting locations on Earth for healing and support, as opposed to personal grids for individual manifestation. It is also beneficial to consider awareness of the many different methods of energy healing, as you begin creating and exploring specific gridwork missions.

This is the evolutionary path of the gridworker; to begin with the personal and expand into the global. Everyone has a different, unique journey, and as multi-dimensional consciousness comes more and more online, it brings a greater awareness that very often expands into the recognition of responsibility toward others. For those who feel called to work with Earth Energy, this translates into a desire to get out into nature and act on behalf of the planet. Six months ago, this was me.

The first crystal grid that I planted was very basic. It was just four points, representing the four cardinal directions; North, South, East and West. The evening before my planned expedition, I drove to Keene; a quiet, college town in New Hampshire that was not far from Mount Monadnock. I had chosen Monadnock because it fell along the same coordinates as many other sacred sites in Western Massachusetts, near where I live. I wanted to activate the Earth Energy lines and strengthen the land health. The next morning, I climbed the mountain, found a sheltered location off the beaten path near the summit, and quite awkwardly did my work. Exactly twelve hours (to the minute) later, a small plane crashed into a building a few doors down from the bed and breakfast where I had spent the night. It was a very potent message from the Universe. This was my awakening of my own sacred mission here on Earth, and I became highly motivated to continue.

If you feel called in this way, start where you are. Tune in to subtle impressions, and that way that they make you feel. Is there a particular spot out in Nature that calls to you, giving you awareness of a special connection between you and the land? If you've always been fascinated by a particular location, either because of the energetic impressions that you pick up while you are there, or because of your knowledge about a certain history, pay attention. This connection is a great starting point for gridwork. It is always an important thing to consider the attunement that you have to the land; this has already set up a resonance that will help the gridwork process. Tap into it intuitively during meditation and see what impressions you come up with. In the very beginning, I started exploring grid work in just this way, because I felt such a strong pull to a certain area near where I live. The Monadnock trip was meant to be a practice run.

For many years, I have loved to drive out to different trails across Western Massachusetts and go on hiking expeditions. Mount Tom in Holyoke has long been my favorite hiking spot; this is the highest peak in a hundred-mile-long ridge known as the Metacomet, which extends north to Vermont and south to the Long Island Sound. The many miles of terrain have countless trails, some more well-traveled than others, and an interesting history. It was once the site of a well-known amusement park, Mountain Park; a popular destination for thrill seekers from the surrounding areas in New York, Massachusetts, Connecticut, New Hampshire and Vermont for almost a hundred years. Mount Tom's popularity gradually increased beginning in the late 1800s, when the Holyoke Street Railway Company built a trolley park as part of a destination resort area. The trolley station was converted into Mountain Park Amusement Park not long after. Despite several devastating fires, the park remained in operation until the late 1990s, when a final, massive fire caused so much widespread damage that the park was abandoned. The historic carousel was moved to the center of Holyoke where it continues to operate, thanks to a Foundation dedicated to its preservation. I have always been very

drawn to carousels and Ferris wheels, and now that I
have become attuned to Earth Energies, I have come to
realize that it is because they are material representations
of Star gate power. They are erected on highly charged
locations, and they activate portals. The mountain itself,
now a designated State Park, is largely used by hikers
and nature lovers, and some ruined foundations of an
Alpine Slide, and various buildings still dot the
mountainous landscape.

I never visited Mountain Park as a child, never
rode the trolleys, and never saw Mount Tom in its
heyday, yet it has always fascinated me. Since my very
first hike up to the summit some thirty years ago, I was
acutely aware of the powerful Earth Energies emanating
from this sacred place. Conversations with other
psychically-sensitive people in the area confirmed that
this awareness was shared by many local community
members. I was conscious of a very strong pull to plant a
crystal grid pattern at the summit of the mountain, and as
I enlisted the help of a like-minded friend and we began

doing gridwork, the project expanded. Within two weeks, we had established a trifecta of crystal grids on three separate peaks of the mountain, and had traveled the entire base of the mountain, planting thirteen additional crystal points. We were highly motivated to finish this work before winter froze the ground solid, the way that it typically does in New England. As I was planning out the work to be done, I was also busy researching the specific details about the history of the mountain to broaden my knowledge. The more that I learned, the greater my existing connection to the land was amplified. This is part of the process! Immersion with the energetic land signatures and structures thereon, as well as a more formal study of the ley lines, nodes, and sacred sites which affect the areas leads to intuitive knowing of how to proceed; this is truly what is meant by growing into one's power. With time, people find that they can sense land trauma that is locked in place by the structures placed on it, such as recognition of what is happening with the Revolutionary War monuments that commemorate historic battle sites.

Early on and shortly after I first acquired my Vogel crystal, I began charting latitude and longitude of various other sites around Western Massachusetts on a map that I created, tuning in to places that I had visited and felt an energetic connection with. Quickly, I realized that these areas of benevolent energy all fall within one degree of each other on the grid coordinate system that runs through the 42nd Parallel. Here in Western Massachusetts, there are many other places of power that fall in and very close to this energy line. Detroit, Michigan also plugs into this channel, well-known for its occult signature. Detroit is a place where numerous places of power that were recognized and utilized by Indigenous American tribal people have been siphoned and blocked with implant technologies and symbolism, particularly by the military industrial complex.

Mapping the areas and looking for patterns, I grew more and more intrigued. I began to develop a plan to visit these areas in the coming year to establish crystal grids to help strengthen and direct the existing organic grid signatures. After Mount Monadnock, the weather held out long enough to allow me to set up six other crystal grids, including several on my family's lands before it became too cold. As I worked, and my plans evolved, so did my familiarity with the different crystals, and my knowledge of energy healing modalities that I began thinking about incorporating into the work. I felt the momentum that was building and building, and I did not want to stop or be limited by the weather. So, as the Northeast winter months rolled in and the freezing nights prevented any more in-ground work outside, I began exploring remote gridwork.

CHAPTER TWELVE: REMOTE GRIDWORKING

One of the most potent and all-encompassing realizations to come into mainstream awareness over the last fifty or so years is the power of the Quantum Field. The covid era greatly accelerated this evolution in ways that no one could have possibly predicted. Gridworking has taken on an entirely new dimension from the way it used to be; it has gone global. Groups of lightworkers have been joining each other in remote missions, using meditation, remote viewing, and energy work that targets distant locations. Depending upon the location, the intentions are often to amplify and support places of power, to cleanse and clear inversions, to release trapped earthbound traumas and to heal the land and all life on it. While physically traveling to Giza or Machu Picchu for in-person DNA star gate activation is the experience of a lifetime, the power of the Quantum really has no limits. Massive changes can and do occur, simply through intention. The possibilities that remote, virtual missions can explore are endless; this has been a truly epic gift that the covid era gave to the world. Remote gridworking "containers" have the advantage of allowing like-minded people from across the world to meet virtually and to journey together in the Quantum field.

Prayer circles and on-line group meditations have shifted energies and affected events on the world stage to the good, particularly in the last three years. When two or more people come together with a shared intention, the power is amplified; when many people come together, the amplification is exponential. There have been numerous reports from different individuals suffering health or personal crises who have been helped by groups of people coming together online for scheduled meditations on their behalf; sometimes the results are quite dramatic. Beyond personal experience, kinesiology has been used to measure how consciousness shifts as a result of applied quantum work. Muscle testing can be done through a number of different methods (swaying and the finger pad test are two examples) to measure changes. A pendulum is another method that is often used to record that actual changes have taken place. On a broader scale, the Schumann Resonance is also a very concrete barometer of positive, permanent changes that have been measured. Since the beginning of 2023, the average frequency that the Schumann has been registering at is 8.35 hertz; this is a significant jump from the 7.83 hertz frequency that has been the average for at least the last thousand years! The effects of keeping people isolated inside their homes, gaining distance from the frantic pace of the matrix hamster wheel were the opposite of what the controllers expected and the last thing that they wanted. Energetic connection and telepathic communication began to flow and to increase naturally, bringing the human collective into greater connectivity with each other, and into a much higher state of consciousness than we have experienced in the past, at an ever-increasing speed. There is no stopping, or going back; we, and the Earth, are ascending.

Entire communities of gridworkers have been coming together into tightly knit groups over the past several years, whereas in years past, solo practitioners tended to do individualized gridwork in the physical. Amanda DeMarco (IndigoAngel222.com), Ashayana Deane (ArhAyas Productions LLC) and the Foundation for Science and Spirituality (fssuniverse.org) are a few examples of teachers and groups who have developed helpful guidance for gridworkers, and they continue to teach and train like-minded people across the world, targeting planetary grid healing. Information about their work, their missions, and ways to reach them can be found through a simple internet search. Amanda DeMarco is a particularly inspiring teacher and mentor. She has been instrumental in bringing a level of focus and professionalism to remote gridworking, and is one of the pioneers in this newly-expanding field. In the last several years, she has traveled around the world for Star Gate activations, and to live missions in locations where the land has been locked down with inversion technologies, including most recently, the Vatican. In addition to her fearless, boots-on-the-ground work, she also hosts remote gridworker missions each month, bringing her community to target locations all around the world.

In November of 2022, Amanda launched an intensive course designed to teach others about gridwork facilitation, with an emphasis on remote mission work. I was very excited at the opportunity to absorb her expansive teachings directly, and to receive the benefits of her personal experience. It also gave me the chance to take an active role in one of her gridwork missions. At the same time, I was beginning to create my own practice with my group, developing the process and the flow that felt right for me. I developed my specialized itinerary for remote gridwork missions using Amanda's basic template as the structural foundation, evolving it and personalizing it to my own orientation and gifts.

A gridwork facilitator creates a plan for the mission ahead of time and collaborates with the participants to identify those with specialties who wish to take on various roles during the missions. She determines the flow of the process and the key elements, the landing and extrication sites, and builds the itinerary, sharing it with the members of the group ahead of time so that everyone can get an idea of what to expect during the session. She plots the specific target points out on a map and provides visuals so that as she is leading the mission, she can pull up pictures of the locations, symbols, and other helpful foci for people as they are going through the process of journeying together. Generally, she will also create a crystal grid in her home before the mission begins, to help establish the container of psychic protection for the group. She will schedule the virtual meeting, invite the participants, and set up the room to ensure that it is a safe and secure space for the work.

Remote gridwork missions can be as simple or as complicated as the gridwork facilitator wishes to make them; the most important element of the entire process is, again, the intention. When groups of people come together with a shared intention to do healing work, there is great power, and even the most stoic of traditional practitioners have found that virtual therapy and healing sessions are every bit as effective as being in the room with the person receiving the work. One of the beautiful lessons that came out of the covid era was the realization of just how connected we all are on the quantum, energetic level. Remote group gridwork is no exception; Earth Energies can be felt and worked with quantumly.

The possibilities that creativity and intuition can design are boundless whenever the intention to take responsibility as stewards of the Earth is realized. All that is required is willingness to act and openness to learn. Many, many people find that they are called strongly to this work, and often all that is needed is the simple awareness of an opportunity to participate. This can be the necessary first step that, once taken, brings a recognition that gridworking is a personal mission that one has come here to do.

CHAPTER THIRTEEN: FIRST REMOTE MISSION

Energy healing can release the energetic trauma trapped in the cellular body of the land, and free up the higher consciousnesses of sovereignty and freedom that were the signatures of the living men and women whose actions created the Union of organic states known as America. The very first remote gridwork mission that I developed and then facilitated for my new team was created with the intention of releasing the trauma locked into the land from the battlefields in Lexington and Concord.

I could feel how the spirit of freedom and sovereignty which sparked the American Revolution surging from the Boston area of Massachusetts in 1776 had been very much absent in American consciousness for a long time. This lack is a yawning void that has been growing, becoming more pronounced. The covid era was a lesson in providing clarity through contrast. The behavior of a large part of the population in its willing acceptance of government tyranny revealed that these essential human energies were being actively blocked and suppressed.

I chose this itinerary first, because I knew that at the time that I was planning the mission, astrologically we were at the cusp of the Pluto return, which was bringing back this most powerful of planetary influences to the exact point where it was two hundred and fifty years ago. It was very relevant to me, living here in Massachusetts where the first shots of the Revolutionary War were fired, particularly given my family lineage. My mother is an Allen, descended from Ethan Allen's Green Mountain Boys legacy, so American patriotism runs through my blood. The oppressive environment created by the ever-increasing weight of governmental overreach that grew from the covid era is the antithesis of everything America stands for. All of Massachusetts has been heavily affected. It was a very fitting mission, and five of my friends agreed.

I began by clarifying my intentions for this mission, and detailed the astrological influences and natural energies that were prevalent at the time as I began building my itinerary. I did some research online into Boston and the Revolutionary War, looking at maps and photographs of historical sites. As I was researching, many insights came to me about specific areas; the war trauma that was held in place by the monuments installed on Lexington Green, and Bunker Hill, and also the stale, dormant energy in the Old North Church, from which the famous two lanterns had been hung to give the signal "two if by sea". I thought about the famous Green Dragon Tavern, which had been the meeting place for the patriots. The original tavern burned down in 1832, and now only a single plaque marks where it once stood.

I could intuitively feel that these two locations contained powerful energy that had gone inert and were just waiting to be reactivated. The flames of freedom needed to burn once more from the church's belfry windows. Additionally, as I reflected on the area, I considered the area where the Boston Brahmins had concentrated themselves from America's early days and set up their control system. This legacy is now a vast spiderweb, and it continues to inflict experimentation, victimization and medical tyranny across the entire world; symbolized in the institution called Harvard. With my third eye, I saw clearly that this was the location of the "new" England Monarchy Seal, and the inverted serpent sigil of power; the Caduceus staff. True students of the esoteric are fully aware of how this double-serpent symbol of commercialism and deception has hijacked the Rod of Asclepius, who represents true healing energy.

Finally, I considered the Star Fort Independence, located just outside of the city at the edge of Boston Harbor, and intuited how this area with its powerful Earth Energy was being tapped and drained, keeping open a direct channel between the first Monarchy Seal in the United Kingdom and the second seal located in the United States. The back-and-forth transfer of energy has been ongoing since Harvard was created in the 1600s by the agents of the British Accreditation Registry, otherwise known as the Massachusetts General Court.

The Monarchy Seal is a very powerful occult implant unknowingly carried inside the energetic bodies of nearly all of humanity. It represents the enslavement of all peoples who have fallen under dictatorial rule of queens, kings, emperors, pharaohs, and chieftains down through the ages; every new monarch reinforces this energy of servitude and adds a new layer to the implant. Understandably, it is very thick in the individual's biofield template and creates a massive blockage that prevents people from accessing the energies of freedom and self-sovereignty. Numerous forces have been at play here in Massachusetts, to suppress, control and siphon life-force energy, and the effects are amplified out across the entire grid.

All of these things are occurring outside of the perception of most people who are going about their day to day lives, yet the evidence is right there. The old

North Church, Paul Revere's home, and other places where the energetic birthplace of the American spirit have been encapsulated and prevented from breathing. They are surrounded by commercialism on all sides. Only tiny patches of land and soil can still be found in the city of Boston, and the majority of these are historic cemeteries, kept free of weeds by pesticide applications that continually poison the Earth there. Slowly, historical buildings created with artistry have been replaced by sharp-angled windowed structures that are as hideous as they are soulless. Gentrification has all but eliminated entire populations of vibrant people who once were the living heartbeat of the city. Only those who are in relentless pursuit of wealth can now afford to live and spend time there. Boston has even harbored an unapprehended gang of serial murderers over the last several decades; the Smiley Faced Killers. These are all signs that the land here is in a state of dis-ease; a place where the artificiality of anti-life energy flourishes and preys upon organic life.

I meditated on the specific locations that were tied closely to the American Revolution, intuitively finding the root of the inversions and energy hijacking portals that were going on. From there, I created detailed affirmations of intention to correct them in the targeted areas section of the itinerary. Then I searched for a landing and extrication location near Boston that would serve as the remote gathering place for the group; I was called immediately to the Marblehead Lighthouse, some thirty miles away. This particular location holds a very special significance for me. It was the last place that I visited with my twin flame during our final motorcycle ride as a couple just before our breakup, and the photo that he had taken of it, all lit up at twilight, is one of my favorite pictures. It represents a beautiful, peaceful sanctuary, and a beacon of powerful and beneficial energy. Lighthouses mark energy vortex points; they stand at the convergence of Earth, air and water.

This location also played an important role in the Revolutionary War, as the Marblehead Regiment was a force to be reckoned with and was very influential to America winning its freedom. I have used this same location as the landing spot for many subsequent remote gridwork missions to Eastern Massachusetts. Each time, the connection grows, and the Earth Energy in that area on the coast becomes a little bit stronger and more focused.

I completed the itinerary, developing my own opening prayer, unity vow and prayer of protection. I detailed the work that needed to be done at the specific locations we would be viewing remotely and targeting, building in all the impressions that had come to me through my third eye; specific inversions needing corrections and dark portals needing clearing. I also collaborated with my team to find out about their psychic tools, and guardian creatures and energies that resonated with them. Additionally, I needed to know who wanted to take on specific roles during the mission. I built all of these pieces directly into the Itinerary.

I shared the completed itinerary with my team, asking for input. Normally, this isn't necessary, however at the time, none of us had participated in any type of remote gridwork mission before and none of us knew what to expect. It felt like a good idea to see if others had strong feelings about what would or would not potentially work.

I then charted the coordinates on a map using Scribblesmaps.com. Each of the targeted locations, from the lighthouse to the battlefields, to the buildings could be seen in the context of a zoomed-out map that showed the entire terrain and the relation of one location to the next. This software is very helpful in laying out visual patterns that very often reveal geometric shapes and occult symbols which have been running behind the scenes affecting the flow of Earth Energies in the area.

Finally, I set up the tabs on my browser to bring up a picture of each of the locations during the mission. I had to do this planfully, so that the sequence of each of the target sites was accurate. I wanted to ensure that during the actual mission, it would be effortless for me to simply click through each of the sites as we were focusing on it. This was a visual tool that I felt would strongly influence our ability to concentrate our intentions.

I sent out invitations by email to each of my team members and set up a physical crystal grid in my bedroom using a flower of eternal life pattern laid over a map of Massachusetts. When the time drew near to open the virtual room, I was already set up.

None of us knew what to expect, and as even the idea of gridworking was a completely foreign concept to half of the group, I facilitated the entire process with the help of just one other person. This was the friend who had accompanied me across Mount Tom planting crystals. She was a sound frequency healer and brought her tuning forks to the mission. She was also very used to leading guided meditations for large groups, and had a strong I Am Presence, so she had volunteered to take on the major role of leading the group while I juggled the technical, visual presentation so that people could see each location, and the map.

The mission took just over an hour. We had technical difficulties, and the only transformational tools that people were aware of (other than the Blue Flame, which is my own personal tool) were basic and/or traditional. Several people couldn't identify with any magical creature. Several were more traditionally religious and so the entire concept was brand new. At the end, everyone was absolutely thrilled that they had participated, and felt that she had given her all. People reported that they had been able to feel intuitively through the entire journey, and had been very plugged in. We knew that we had done something massive in the energetic realms. Everyone was excited about the next mission, which we decided would be targeting Salem, Massachusetts for healing and restoration of the residual trauma from the Salem Witch Trial era.

The process of developing our first remote gridwork mission was a wonderful learning experience for all of us. We learned of things that we wanted to change for the next time, and what had worked very well. The group praised the use of visuals; the tabs showing each targeted location had made it very easy for people to view them remotely. They also loved the Scribblesmaps application.

We couldn't wait for our next journey the following month. A new community of gridworkers was born.

CHAPTER FOURTEEN: LIVE MISSION TO THE MOTHER ARC STAR GATE

The astrological energies coming in from the lineup of so many planets populating the same quadrant of the sky beginning in March of 2023 were immense. With the advent of eclipse season, this was a powerful and transformational time. I had been waiting for the weather to warm up enough to be able to resume crystal gridwork on the land and planned to take a road trip down to Staten Island, New York to find the Mother Arc Star Gate portal there and activate it with a crystal grid.

The Mother Arc Star Gates are part of the planetary grid system that holds the frequency of the Blue Ray of Creation and reconnects the original organic Sophianic Divine Mother principle that has been hijacked, suppressed and distorted here on Earth for eons. Its manipulation has allowed for continuing distortion of the Divine Father archetype into its shadow; the toxic masculine. An important part of the soul mission known as the twin flame journey is to heal and restore these two archetypes to their original, Divine blueprint.

Mother Arcs are not part of the original planetary star gate system; they were created later, as part of the ascension rescue mission. They are keyed to the DNA of the Blue Rays and of the Indigos who originate from galaxies and worlds far away in the multi-verse. These being can activate the gates to assist Earth and all of humanity. (Ascensionglossary.com).

Ever since my awakening to the mission of Blue Flame guardianship, I felt pulled toward this star gate. That this location was the site of a planned six hundred thirty-foot tall Ferris wheel that had been announced in 2012 was very telling, and I knew intuitively that the blueprint for the Ferris wheel was right where we would find the Mother Arc.

On Good Friday, April 7th, my sister and I took a road trip with the same close friend who had helped with the Mount Tom trifecta, down to Staten Island. The drive was about two and a half hours, and we found the site with ease. Staten Island has an interesting history. One of the oldest military forts in America is located here; Fort Wadsworth, and it was visible from the highway as we came down the off-ramp. It was here that the final shot of the American Revolution was fired by a departing British Ship of War in November of 1783. The Island had housed many Tories during the War, and most of them left the area after it ended. By 1955, the Island became the site of the largest landfill in the world; Fresh Kills, an area that had once been a tidal wilderness area teeming with wildlife and a cleansing salt marsh. Since its opening in 1948, the landfill was rigorously protested by the residents of the Island, and this played a large part in a majority bid for the Island's succession from New York City proper in the early 1990s.

I learned of Staten Island's connection to the Revolutionary War after we had returned from our mission to plant the crystal grid. I found it fascinating that the first remote gridwork mission that I chose for my team included the site where the first shots signaling the start of the Revolutionary War were fired; Lexington. Now, the first in-person gridwork mission of 2023, three months later, happened to be where the shots signaling its end were fired. It was a strange coincidence.

The crystal layout that I had chosen for this was the aqua, twelve-point pattern within the picture that I had found on Lisa Renee's website which represented the Mother Arc. The centering stone was a rose quartz pyramid; I chose this because of this stone's special connection to the heart chakra, which felt very fitting as the primary energy that we were activating with this grid was the Divine Mother principle of love. This area really needed to have the 528 hertz frequencies of love anchored here. The second layer of the grid consisted of twelve Herkimer diamonds; the stones of attunement, their high-vibrational consciousness, was charged to magnify the principle of Divine love out across the land. Six blue topaz and six amethysts were the next layer. Amethyst is a powerful stone of healing, and blue topaz is a stone that is tuned to the frequency of the Blue Flame of Creation. This crystal has always been my favorite stone, and one which I have felt a special connection to. Finally, the last layer consisted of four tiger eyes, to strengthen the root and sacral chakras; four citrine quartz crystals to empower the solar plexus chakra, and four lapis crystals for third eye awakening.

The location directly where the Star Gate sits was not accessible. The entire area was a construction site, and it was sectioned off by barriers. However, a walkway above it provided us with an excellent location amongst the roots of a hollowed-out tree. The day was cold and brisk, and there were very few people out and about; we were able to lay out the grid without worrying about curious onlookers until we reached the final layer of crystals.

As we placed the citrine quartzes in the four directions, a man approached us, yelling to himself and gesturing with his arms in the air. He was clearly in a state of severe mental incoherence and was weaving his way towards where we were working at a fast clip.

Hastily, we positioned the lapis crystals, then activated the grid with our Vogel crystals. We covered the spot with soil and quickly patted it down firmly to hide all signs that it had ever been disturbed. Then we moved away and headed toward the car, deciding not to attempt the final thirteen points around the outer edges. We could feel the energy activating around us, and we knew that what we had done was effective.

From inside the car, we watched the man as he stopped just beside the tree. He looked all around….and then, visibly calmed down. He did not touch the tree, or attempt to uncover the dirt at its base, which hid the crystal grid. He simply stood beside it for a moment, then slowly turned around and began walking back in the direction that he had come in, this time quietly.

We drove home, feeling energized and elated, all the while visualizing Earth Energies radiating out into the surrounding lands, healing and transforming the people there. And that night, there were videos of colored orbs in the sky above New York City being circulated all over the internet by many people.

CHAPTER FIFTEEN: CONCLUSION

The implications of all that has been discussed are immense, as are the number of resources that can help an individual grid worker embark upon a lifelong journey of learning about the Earth's multi-dimensional grid.

Energy healing, both in the physical and in the Quantum, has enormous potential to heal the Earth much the same way that it heals humans and animals. Her physical and energetic template is a macrocosm of our own energetic, human blueprint. Our solutions for detoxification, healing and recovery support, when expanded, provide a pathway toward assisting her to detoxify, heal and recover also; and in the same multi-dimensional way that we understand what applies to our own energy bodies. Spiritual and energetic healing methods and quantum entrainment, concepts that we are only beginning to fully comprehend, are as relevant to Earth as they are to humanity. What now must come is our ability to fully integrate and learn how to communicate consciously with her as we begin practicing these different modalities and techniques in service to her. She is much vaster than we are; our one voice becomes a million voices in the unified, all encompassing-ness that is as Nature, however with our increasing understanding of our own biological and energetic templating, we integrate more and greater comprehension of hers. With time, as more and more of us immerse ourselves in this work, we begin the process of reestablishing the lines of communication that we have lost touch with. As our physical and energetic bodies begin to re-align, we also begin to move back into coherence and harmonious synchronization of the frequencies and rhythms of Earth Energy. This in turn raises our consciousness and increases our connection to Source, bringing us that much closer to our own ascension.

As Above, So Below is a Hermetic maxim that spans multiple dimensions, and it is a truth that applies to all beings on Earth, with respect to our individual and our collective relationships with the planet herself. Just as we ground ourselves into our own physical bodies; a macrocosm, we ground ourselves to the physical manifestation of our Divine Mother here in this reality; Earth. The energetic channels that make up our human blueprint and create the many levels of consciousness that reflect our divine lineage are mirrored in the energetic channels that make up the blueprint of Earth. We are all intricately connected, and interdependent. It has become very evident that the farther away we have moved as a society from our connection to Earth, the more we have become disconnected from Source. Whether we wish to admit it or not, our survival as a race is dependent upon our planet, both spiritually and architecturally. "There is an intimate connection between the time portal system and the genetic code of all life forms within it. When the time portals are damaged the genetic imprint of biological life is altered, mutated from its original pattern." (Deane, 2002, p 127).

Responsibility is a key lesson of the newly transitioning Age of Aquarius, and as this truth grows within the family of man's collective consciousness, so gradually do memories stored within those fragmented-but-still-energetically-present DNA. The "original Keylonta Code patterns were left within the cellular imprint so that once your species had evolved into cognition of its true lineage you would have with you the original codes needed to reassemble your connection to the original Soul Matrix." (Deane, 2002, p 157). A 2020 University of Cambridge study found healthy, viable four-stranded DNA in human cells; this supports that we are indeed recovering our memories. Earth's memories, and our simultaneous transmutations of the distortions. (Hooper, 2020).

Here on the three-dimensional Earth plane, we exist in dense physicality, and therefore physical action is necessary and indeed it is the very process of taking action that assists the overall process. Working with the Earth's grid, we bring our intentions to heal and restore into manifestation. We have a duty to act, and in the action, we catalyze change.

With interest and exploration, it is not difficult to find extensive work of researchers, historians and scientists who have recognized their missions as relating to Earth Energies and conscious technologies from a variety of different perspectives, and numerous resources are available both in print, and online. A great many people who are intentionally conducting group workshops in person and remotely to heal and strengthen the Earth's grid showcase their work entirely through practice that is memorialized in video recordings and live communities. These resources are not detailed here in this work; however, these contemporary practitioners are a presence that is both powerful and growing. Several of them have been referenced within the body of this documentary, as their important work is helping to raise the frequency of the collective consciousness on the planet at this time and they have valuable information to share with the world. We are at a time now where discernment is more important than anything else; the old, inverted matrix systems which only view "credentials" and authority outside of us as valid are being increasingly discarded as people reclaim their sovereignty and power, recognizing the authenticity of their own inner knowing (clair-cognizance in particular, although the other clairs are equally valid and may be stronger, depending upon the individual). A great deal of information comes to us through dreams and through synchronicities, all of which are messages from the Divine. There are many, many resources available and the maxim "take what you can use and let the rest go", in the immortal words of Ken Kesey's *One Flew Over the Cuckoo's Nest*, applies profoundly to our individual and collective journey(s) of evolution.

Namaste, starborn brothers and sisters; we are all Soul Family

IN GRATITUDE, THE FOLLOWING ARE CITED:

About Marcel Vogel and his work. Marcelvogellegacy.com. https://marcelvogellegacy.com/about-marcel-vogel

Askinosie, H. *(2023). How to Make Your Own Crystal Grid.* Energymuse.com. https://energymuse.com/blogs/crystals/crystal-grids

Besser, B. P. (2007), Synopsis of the historical development of Schumann resonances, Radio Science, 42, RS2S02, doi:10.1029/2006RS003495

Deane, A. (2002). *Voyagers, The Sleeping Abductees Volume 1 of the Emerald Covenant CDT Plate-Translations.* Wild Flower Press.

Childress, D. H & Clendenon, B. (2000). *Atlantis and the Power System of the Gods.* Adventures Unlimited Press. Kempton, IL.

Coons, R. (2009). *Earth Chakras: A Definitive Guide.* Self-Published by Robert Coons, distributed by Lulu.

Demarco, A. *(2021, October 20). Lunar Stargate Planetary Locations.* Indigoangel222.com. https://www.indigoangel222.com/post/lunar-stargate-planetary-locations-1

Duff, R. (2023). *A Guide to Leylines, Earth Energies, Nodes & Large Vortexes, 2nd Edition.* Self-Published by Rory Duff.

Dwoskin, H. (2007). *The Sedona Method, Your Key to Lasting Happiness, Success, Peace and Emotional Well-Being.* Sedona Press, Sedona, AZ.

Fogg, K. (2018). Crystal Gridwork: The Power of Crystals and Sacred Geometry to Heal, Protect and Inspire. Red Wheel/Weiser. Newburyport, MA.

Hawkins, D. R. (1995). Power Versus Force The Hidden Determinants of Human Behavior. Hay House. New South Wales.

Hooper, R. (2020, July 20). *Quadruple-stranded DNA seen in healthy human cells for the first time.* NewScientist.com. https://www.newscientist.com/article/2249390-quadruple-stranded-dna-seen-in-healthy-human-cells-for-the-first-time/

Igan, M. (2010). *Earth's Forbidden Secrets Part 1, Searching for the Past.* Independent Publishing; Self-Published by Max Igan.

Mckusick, E. (2021). *Tuning the Human Biofield, 2nd Edition.* Inner Traditions Bear and Company. Rochester, NY.

Michell, J. (1975). *The Earth Spirit.* Crossroad Publishing. New York, NY.

Michell, J. (1973). *The View Over Atlantis.* Abacus Edition; Sphere Books, Ltd. London.

Mindvibrations. (2023). The Ancient Solfeggio Scale Explained.

https://www.mindvibrations.com/ancient-solfeggio-scale/

Nelson, B. (2019). *The Emotion Code*. St. Martin's Press, New York, NY.

Northrup, C. (2019). *Dodging Energy Vampires An Empath's Guide to Evading Relationships that Drain You and Restoring Your Health and Power.* Hay House Publishing, Australia.

Powell, R. & Bowden, D. (2013). Astrogeographia: Correspondences between the Stars and Earthly Locations, A Bible of Astrology and Earth Chakras. *Journal for Star Wisdom,* pp1-12. http://www.astrogeographia.org/docs/astrogeographia_book/Earth_Chakras.pdf

Quantum Healing Hypnosis Academy. *https://www.dolorescannon.com*

Ra. (1984). *The Law of One: Book One*. Whitford Press. Antglen, PA.

Renee, L. (2013, May 31). *Crystal Caverns. Energy Synthesis Forum.* Ascensionglossary.com. https://ascensionglossary.com/index.php/Crystal_Caverns

Roberts, K. (1953). *The Seventh Sense*. Doubleday & Company, INC. Garden City, NY.

Stargates and Hidden Portals on Earth and in Space. Gaia.com. (2020, November 21). https://www.gaia.com/article/stargates-hidden-portals-earth-space

Stuemke, *C S. Mysterious Star Forts, Stellar Symbols of a Forgotten Past.*

https://chadstuemke.com/mysterious-star-forts-stellar-symbols-of-a-forgotten-past/

The Earth Grid & Gaia. Foundation for Science & Spirituality. (2018, December 5). https://www.fssuniverse.org/

Worley, L. (2021). *Puzzle Pieces to The Cabal, Mind Control, and Slavery.* Puzzle Pieces Together LLC, United States.

APPENDIX: PAST REMOTE ITINERARIES

The following section includes the Itineraries from live and remote gridwork missions that took place from January through April of 2023. Much appreciation and thanks go to Amanda J. DeMarco (IndigoAngel), who provided the inspiration for the format, which was taken and then developed into my own personal and make my own in my remote gridwork missions. These pages reflect the journey of evolution that we traveled as the process improved and transformed with each subsequent mission. Feel free to take and use in your own work, as it applies.

MISSION ONE: JANUARY, 2023

PROJECT SPIRIT OF 1776

<u>**Outline and Itinerary for Group Gridwork**</u> –

Boston/Lexington/Concord Massachusetts

<u>**Shared Intention:**</u> We come together with our individual gifts and strengths in Service to Others and In Service to Truth; united in a shared mission to work with Earth to heal and restore all life to original, organic perfect Kristos blueprint. Together as one, we bring forth the highest intention to release and transmute all inversions, to free trapped souls, assist their healing and support their journey home to Source, to strengthen and amplify the organic grid, and to assist mankind in restoring memory, Sovereignty, Higher Consciousness and Divine responsibility.

<u>Prayer of Invocation:</u> "Creator of All Beings, Creator of All Beings, Creator of All Beings, Creator of All Love, Creator of all Light, Creator of all Consciousness; Twelve Archangels, always Loyal to the Creator; Magical Creatures, our companions and protectors; Guides, Teachers and Fellow Guardians of our planet's Grid, we come together as sovereign beings, united as brothers and sisters. Our mission is ancient, as Keepers of the Sacred Flames of Creation and protectors of Earth, to work with her to heal and restore the land that we love, and all living soulful beings to the original, organic Kristos blueprint. In perfect love and perfect trust, we stand unified; one Heart, one Mind, and one Spirit and bring forth the highest intention to release all inversions, assist trapped, disconnected souls to heal and find their way home to Source, and to support the family of man in its individual and collective journey back to Sovereignty, Divine Purpose, Higher Consciousness, Responsibility and Remembrance of our true histories and Eternal Role as Stewards of Earth. We ask for assistance, and protection, and we proclaim our intention and combined work is magnified to the power and purity of the Highest Emanation of Original Source. Only that which is in our highest, best good may be present in our circle; our Free Will is Absolute. And So It Is."

<u>Astrological Influences & Current Energies:</u>

December planetary influences -Pluto begins its return to the 1776 cosmic placement, Jupiter has returned to Aries (ruled by Mars); focus on initiative, independence, courage. Full wolf moon in Cancer Friday, January 6th, 2023 – sacral chakra, life force; focus on protection, nurturing, and deep spirituality. New month symbolizes new starts, planets going direct, moving forward with fierce energy and courage and willingness to assume responsibility; excellent planetary influences to restore the energy of Massachusetts, the seat of the Revolution, back to the power, responsibility and resolve embodied by our Founders and overthrow of control matrix.

- Introduction of participants

Guidelines: Our purpose in coming together is to combine the power of our shared energy and gifts in a focused and intentional way, so that the results of our work are amplified and radiate out across Earth's grid in every direction. Attention, Coherence and Purity and respect for each other are all necessary, and for these to be achieved, each of us must come forward from a place of balance and inner harmony.   Please take a moment to find your center before coming to the group, and if necessary, attend to any needed deeper clearing work prior. We will open the session with a group meditation.

Recommended Preparations prior to Group Work:
Please take care to ground yourself and be well-hydrated prior to the start of our mission! We will do short grounding meditation when we come together, however the first layer is important before you arrive.

- A grounding meditation

- Maharic shield activation (Akasha or Merkaba visualization)
- Chakra crystal induction

<u>Virtual Room Etiquette:</u> Virtual work has the potential for technology challenges, so please bring your sense of humor and patience to every session! Other than this, please help to ensure that this is a safe space where all are free to share their authentic selves without judgement and have the opportunity to speak. Kindly push the "raise your hand" button on the app (or, show your raised hand on camera) so that I can call on you to give your input. Kindly keep your microphone muted if you are in a place where there are sound distractions and during times called for in the session.

- At each location/sacred site, we will have group remote viewing, discussion time, keys, sweeps, clarion calls, calling in of transmutative tools, recite prayers, collapse portals, extract negative energies, utilize transformation tools, recite prayers and activations.

<u>Starborn Key – As we set our intentions in preparation to begin our work:</u>

<u>Person Recites:</u> "When we connect together, standing in a circle of the solar cross and holding space of the four directions North/South/East/West with the Four Pillars of Man....we stand as the embodied Spirit of truth of the Universal Divine Plan. We come forth now to prepare this land and work with the true and original Guardians to open the inverted gates for restoration and healing. The way forward is the way of Truth.   We now set the Merkabah at our feet, and see each point of the Merkabah light up as we count 12,11, 10, 9, 8, 7, 6, 5, 4, 3, 2, 1." (Each person calls out a number). We Speak the Way and the Way is Open; and So It is.

<u>Starborn Sweep:</u> When called upon by two or more group members, participants with clearing/restorative gifts (sound healing- tuning forks/bowls, light language, Sigil scrying, crystal consciousness et al) activate and "sweep" across the terrain to empower and clear the grids. This should not be used during remote viewing or navigating the grids, or occur during group discussions/ discovery/ facilitator guidance.

<u>Starborn Oracle:</u> If your gift is tarot/oracle; for deeper insight into the energies of the grids/sacred sites as we experience them, please call out Oracle before/after a sweep to bring through your message.

<u>Starborn Clarion Call:</u> This is a request to call out the tools that you are using, in order to deal with and address whatever elements and issues you are feeling confronted with in this moment.

<u>**TransformationTools to Use:**</u> **(add to list as personal tools of individual Team are brought forward)**

Blue Flame Staff of Power

Golden love light from Grand Central Sun

Phoenix Fire

Elemental tools – trident, sword, dagger et al

Sigils

<u>**Magical Guardian creatures Call:**</u> This is a call to bring in your companions; Phoenix-finisher, Dragon-protection/creation, Mermaid-sisterhood, pure feminine principal, Feline Familiars- independence and Sovereignty, any others to assist and protect.

<u>**Fear Removal Vow**</u> – Use at specific locations and also when fear may be triggered; "Dark to Light! I Am The I Am, and I invoke the Diamond Crystal Light of Source Consciousness to fill our energy bodies and fill this Sacred Space, transmuting all fear programs into pure light and eternal love, dissolving all blockages. I

transmute my fear of ____ and release it into the Light. I
ask that my Teams focus on their spiritual, mental,
etheric and emotional bodies and remove any and all
fear-based programs (here other team members speak up
to identify specific fears). I call upon Source to install
the lattice work of light, swan grid, dove grid, 144,000
Krystos templating into our one shared cosmic mind grid
field and emotional field to remove all fear- based
programs and artificial programs. And So It Is!"

Unity Vow: To be used whenever incoherent or
conflicting energies are present among the group, or
when infiltration is detected; returns attention (and
Intention) to the shared mission of Unity. "Warriors of
divine mission, Guardians of the Sacred Flame, we are
Soul Family from across all cosmic nations and creeds,
and I call upon you now to ReUnite in Service to the
Earth, in Service to Others, and in Service to Truth!
Renew now and sustain the divine light within us all;
remember and rededicate to our Sacred Mission. I avow

my dedication to our sacred, shared purpose and do not consent to any artificial and inorganic intentions; I release all incoherence back to Source! And So It Is"

<u>Portal Collapse/Target Locations:</u>   - Numerous technologies have been implanted to lockdown and imprison the powerful energies of sovereignty, courage and freedom and siphon the trauma of battles and solidify Boston Brahman inverted control matrix- Harvard is America's site of the Monarchy Seal. At each location, we will check in with Mother Earth to ensure that we are doing the work that She desires.

- **Boston Harbor** – Asking for Divine intervention and assistance to use our Loving Light Life Force, the Light of Original Source and our Sacred Tools to scan ….…..and remove implants, portal collapse and dissolve, cleanse and detox the water, activate crystal healing, requesting sea creatures (whales and dolphins) to assist, and Merfolk to assist and guard, and place permanent elevator boxes to invite entities and consciousnesses who are through existing in separation to step inside at any time, to let them ride to Archangel Michael to be released back to Source. Speak Ho'oponopono together; I love you, I'm sorry, forgive me, thank you. Portal is closed; PORTAL IS SEALED..

- **North Church** – Beacon of Revolutionary call to action.   Asking for Divine Intervention and assistance.... to portal collapse and dissolution of distortions; reLight the two steeple lanterns with Flame of Creation; Sigil placement and requesting Dragon protection. place permanent elevator boxes to invite entities and consciousnesses who are through existing in separation to step inside at any time, to let them ride to Archangel Michael to be released back to Source. Speak Ho'oponopono together; I love you, I'm sorry, forgive me, thank you. Portal is closed; PORTAL IS SEALED.

- **Castle Island Star Fort – Fort Independence** – Asking for Divine intervention and assistance.... to remove implants and inversions, and channel the organic Krystos frequencies back through the spiral Earth grid; and Sigil placement, and requesting Dragon protection, place permanent elevator boxes to invite entities and consciousnesses who are through existing in separation to step inside at any time, to let them ride to Archangel Michael to be released back to Source. Speak Ho'oponopono together; I love you, I'm sorry, forgive me, thank you. Portal is closed; PORTAL IS SEALED.

- **Green Dragon Tavern, Boston** – Asking for Divine intervention and assistance.....to plant dragon eggs, Sigil placement, and channel the organic Krystos frequencies back through the spiral Earth grid; place permanent elevator boxes to invite entities and consciousnesses who are through existing in separation to step inside at any time, to let them ride to Archangel Michael to be released back to Source. Speak Ho'oponopono together; I love you, I'm sorry, forgive me, thank you. Portal is closed; PORTAL IS SEALED.

- **Minute Man Park, Concord Obelisk-** Asking for Divine intervention and assistance.....to collapse portal and dissolve, use sacred tools to release trapped battle trauma and integrate and elevate the lesson into the collective consciousness to strengthen all of humanity, and seal obelisk to hijacking, place permanent elevator boxes to invite entities and consciousnesses who are through existing in separation to step inside at any time, to let them ride to Archangel Michael to be released back to Source. Speak Ho'oponopono together; I love you, I'm sorry, forgive me, thank you. Portal is closed; PORTAL IS SEALED.

- **Bunker Hill, Boston Obelisk-** Asking for Divine intervention and assistance.....to collapse portal and dissolve, use sacred tools to release trapped battle trauma and integrate and elevate the lesson into the collective consciousness to strengthen all of humanity, and seal obelisk to hijacking, place permanent elevator boxes to invite entities and consciousnesses who are through existing in separation to step inside at any time, to let them ride to Archangel Michael to be released back to Source. Speak Ho'oponopono together; I love you, I'm sorry, forgive me, thank you. Portal is closed; PORTAL IS SEALED.

- **Harvard, Boston –** Asking for Divine intervention and assistance.....to clear the Harvesting Station and remove and destroy with sacred tools the Monarchy Seal, Caduceus network; demon seed implants, slavery yokes, cult mind control programs; medical experimentation, gender confusion principal distortions— free the trapped snakes on the Caduceus and send organic violet flame into and around the Black Cube network (siphoning cubes in Earth's core, the Abaddon StarGate in Iran, the 911 monument; all harvesting stations) and demon seed implants in human collective energy bodies connected to Chakra system; then cleave the Caduceus staff;   Extract Monarchy Seal and burn with dragon and phoenix fire; free the trapped innocents, collapse tunnels and flood filling them with water and with violet flame; channel the organic Krystos frequencies back through the spiral Earth grid; place permanent elevator boxes to invite entities and consciousnesses who are through existing in separation to be transported back to Source, Sigil placement, requesting Sphinx protection. Speak Ho'oponopono together; I love you, I'm sorry, forgive me, thank you. Portal is closed; PORTAL IS SEALED.

- General across the entire State: Reprogram the 5g towers to radiate 528 and 432 hz healing and love frequencies across Massachusetts and New England......place Herkimer diamonds and rose quartz on the outer perimeter of the land, clockwise- charge and radiate through the ley lines of the Grid, activate and send Source Love and Light and the Spirit of Independence and Freedom! Speak Ho'oponopono together; I love you, I'm sorry, forgive me, thank you. Portal is closed; PORTAL IS SEALED..

<u>Landing and Drop-in Zone:</u> Marblehead Light, Marblehead Mass - (appx 35 miles from Harvard)

<u>Extraction:</u> **Same** -- Reseal and declaration of closed portals, Gratitude prayer; and meditation to return home.

<u>**Special Roles and Healing Modalities:**</u>   The following members have agreed to take special roles for this session: (adding roles and members as we go)

- Opening Guided meditation/grounding/focusing intention, Calling in the Guardian Creatures, Fear Removal Prayer and Unity Vow - M
- Invocation prayer and Clarion Call- K
- Key speaker, Remote viewing journey guide- I
- Oracle- currently no Tarot readers
- Protection and sealing Sigils- M
- Healers- I (tuning forks/bowls); J, D, K (crystals)

<u>**Prior to session:**</u>

Participants each prep prior to session (shield, ground, meditate, hydrate!)

Facilitator - Set up sacred space; map of Massachusetts and crystals to lay out in grid pattern

Pictures of each site

Scribblesmap of all points

Picture of monarchy seal

People join freeconf -   Housekeeping, rundown of process, definitions, visuals

Open remote session- verify connectivity/technology, etiquette

Invocation and basic grounding

Opening – guided meditation and aura hypnosis M (not on script) and call in Spirit Guardians

Clarion call/declaration of Sacred Tools & gifts – K

Key Invocation – Merkabah activation - I

Astral Journey/landing to Lighthouse - I

Speaking of the Fear Removal Vow and the Unity Vow – K

Work through the sites – I leads asking if group has input at each location.

Return to Lighthouse Landing site for extrication & Gratitude Prayer- I

After; Participants debrief and address that we really need to ground and surround ourselves with Source Love

Light- be aware of the potential for any psychic anomalies, and ground, shield/protect.

<u>Notes and Discussion after mission</u>: M's internet went down and she was unable to join the meeting; K took over her roles, 6 remaining participants. Navigation tools included Scribblemaps showing all sites locations, and screenshot of each target for a visual to help participants focus.

FOR NEXT MISSION: Change itinerary around for a better flow.

SECOND MISSION: March 13, 2023

PROJECT RELEASING TORTURED SOULS AND HEALING SACRED LAND – Salem, Massachusetts - 03/13/23

Outline and Itinerary for Group Gridwork

Intention: We come together with our individual gifts and strengths in Service to Others and In Service to Truth; united in a shared mission to work with Earth to heal and restore all life to original, organic perfect Kristos blueprint. Together as one, we bring forth the highest intention to release and transmute all inversions, to free trapped souls, assist their healing and support their journey home to Source, to strengthen and amplify the organic grid, and to assist mankind in restoring memory, Sovereignty, Higher Consciousness and Divine responsibility.

<u>**Astrological Influences & Current Events:**</u> **March is a powerful month, astrologically speaking.** Neptune has returned to Pisces, signaling a return to true spirituality and reconnection to the Divine; a cleansing for the trauma and shattering of the illusions in Salem around the commercialization of a hideously tragic history. Saturn moved into Pisces on the 8th, signaling the end of the restrictions on freedom of the last three years. As we move into the second half of March, heading toward the Aries equinox – six planets are in Aries, a powerhouse of initiatory warrior energy to surge forward into new beginnings. Manwe is within 1 degree of Aries, Varda is at the Galactic Center of the galaxy – these two planets operate beyond the confines of time and space, signify light illuminating and disempowering the darkness. Pluto is at a T-square to the nodal axis until November; this is fundamental transformation, shifting of power to the people (happened in 1789-storming the Bastille) and it is moving into Aquarius, signifying the shift into horizontal society favoring freedom and transformation.

Grounding of mystical energies, and a move away from traditional belief systems and into the spiritual and energetic realms; excellent planetary influences to clear Karma, and dispel illusions as well as honoring the Sacred. Power of collective prayer and intention is magnified. Increasing demolition of old-top down structures, and energies in the collective have been turbulent and dense!

<u>Guidelines:</u> Our purpose in coming together is to combine the power of our shared energy and gifts in a focused and intentional way, so that the results of our work are amplified and radiate out across Earth's grid in every direction from Massachusetts; the birthplace of American Sovereignty. Attention, Coherence and Purity and respect for each other are all necessary, and for these to be achieved, each of us must come forward from a place of balance and inner harmony. Please take a moment to find your center before coming to the group, and if necessary, attend to any needed deeper clearing work prior. We will open the session with a group meditation.

<u>Recommended Preparation prior to Group Work:</u>
Please take care to ground yourself and be well-hydrated prior to the start of our mission! We will do short grounding meditation when we come together, however the first layer is important before you arrive.

- A grounding meditation
- Maharic shield activation (Akasha or Merkaba visualization)
- Chakra crystal induction

<u>Online Etiquette:</u> Virtual work has the potential for technological challenges, so please bring your sense of humor and patience to every session! Other than this, please help to ensure that this is a safe space where all are free to share their authentic selves without judgment and to have the opportunity to speak. Kindly push the "raise your hand" button on the app (or, show your raised hand on camera) so that I can call on you to give your input. Kindly keep your microphone muted if you are in a place where there are sound distractions and during times called for in the session.

- At each location/sacred site, we will have group remote viewing, discussion time, keys, sweeps, clarion calls, calling in of transmutative tools, recite prayers, collapse portals, extract negative energies, utilize transformation tools, recite prayers and activations.

<u>Introduction of participants: New members speak, share specialty</u>

<u>Clarion Call:</u> This is a call to declare your tools. As the mission progresses, at any time, a member may announce Clarion Call when members intuit that the current flow of energies calls for the aid of tools. As the mission progresses, if spirit gives you a thought or a vision during the journey, stop and bring it out.

<u>Transformational Tools:</u> (add to list as personal tools of individual Team are brought forward)

Blue Flame, Violet Flame, Gold Flame, White Flame – emanations of Creation Rays from Divine

A Divine blanket of Christ light– (purification, forgiveness, reclamation of the Divine)

Golden love light from Grand Central Sun

Elemental tools –sword, trident, sword, dagger et al - may be connected with Archangels

Sigils

Relics

Phoenix Fire (Fire elements- action)

Wind vortex (removal of blockages)

Double Diamond Sun Body

<u>Definitions/Instructions:</u>

<u>**Sweep:**</u> When called upon by group members, participants with clearing/restorative gifts (sound healing- tuning forks/bowls, light language, Sigil

scrying, crystal consciousness et al) activate and "sweep" across the terrain to empower and clear the grids. This should not be used during remote viewing or navigating the grids, or occur during group discussions/ discovery/ facilitator guidance.

Starborn Oracle: If your gift is tarot/oracle; for deeper insight into the energies of the grids/sacred sites as we experience them, please call out Oracle before/after a sweep to bring through your message. (currently, we don't have anyone in the group for this).

Fear Removal Vow – Use at specific locations and also when fear may be triggered; "Dark to Light! I Am The I Am, and I invoke the Diamond Crystal Light of Source Consciousness to fill our energy bodies and fill this Sacred Space, transmuting all fear programs into pure light and eternal love, dissolving all blockages. I transmute my fear of ____ and release it into the Light. I ask that my Teams focus on their spiritual, mental, etheric and emotional bodies and remove any and all fear-based programs (here other team members speak up to identify specific fears). I call upon Source to install the lattice work of light, swan grid, dove grid, 144,000 Krystos templating into our one shared cosmic mind grid field and emotional field to remove all fear- based programs and artificial programs. And So It Is!"

Unity Vow: To be used whenever incoherent or conflicting energies are present among the group, or when infiltration is detected; returns attention (and Intention) to the shared mission of Unity. "Warriors of divine mission, Guardians of the Sacred Flame, we are Soul Family from across all cosmic nations and creeds, and I call upon you now to ReUnite in Service to the Earth, in Service to Others, and in Service to Truth! Renew now and sustain the divine light within us all; remember and rededicate to our Sacred Mission. I avow my dedication to our sacred, shared purpose and do not

consent to any artificial and inorganic intentions; I
release all incoherence back to Source! And So It Is."

THE MISSION

The Invocation Prayer- K : "Creator of All Beings,
Creator of All Beings, Creator of All Beings, Creator of
All Love, Creator of all Light, Creator of all
Consciousness; Twelve Archangels, always Loyal to the
Creator; Magical Creatures, our companions and
protectors; Guides, Teachers and Fellow Guardians of
our planet's Grid, we come together as sovereign
beings, united as brothers and sisters. Our mission is
ancient, as Keepers of the Sacred Flames of Creation and
protectors of Earth, to work with her to heal and restore
the land that we love, and all living soulful beings to the
original, organic Kristos blueprint. In perfect love and
perfect trust, we stand unified; one Heart, one Mind, and
one Spirit and bring forth the highest intention to release
all inversions, assist trapped, disconnected souls to heal

and find their way home to Source, and to support the family of man in its individual and collective journey back to Sovereignty, Divine Purpose, Higher Consciousness, Responsibility and Remembrance of our true histories and Eternal Role as Stewards of Earth. We ask for assistance, and protection, and we proclaim our intention and combined work is magnified to the power and purity of the Highest Emanation of Original Source. Only that which is in our highest, best good may be present in our circle; our Free Will is Absolute. And So It Is."

<u>Journey Activation Key – D-</u> "We connect together, standing in a circle of the solar cross and holding space of the four directions North/South/East/West with the Four Pillars of Mankind, grounding and activating the Diamond Crystal Earth Core, Diamond Crystal Sea Waters and Diamond Mother disks running through the glaciers of Antarctica to expand the double diamond crystal fabrics through all organic grids. We stand as the embodied Spirit of truth of the Universal Divine Plan, inheritors of the original divine peace and freedom earth template, and we call forth the pure plasma Founder Flames of Divine Emanation into the inversion Matrix in Salem to the core of the Black Cube network to transform and overpower the channels with Divine Source frequencies. We come forth now to prepare this land and work with the true and original Guardians to open the inverted gates for restoration and healing, activating the Krystos and Sophianic Energies and clear trapped misery, trauma, victimization, fear, persecution and suffering and releasing the lessons of Unity and forgiveness for Humanity's ascension. The dove grid is now activated with the olive branch codes; come forth now and clear this land and all nations, merging the fields of peace, freedom and liberation. The way forward is the way of Truth. We now set the Merkabah at our feet and see each point of the Merkabah light up as we count 12,11, 10, 9, 8, 7, 6, 5, 4, 3, 2, 1." (Each member calls a number). We Speak the Way and the Way is Open-and So It is!

<u>Guided Meditation/Remote travel to landing zone – Marblehead Lighthouse – K</u> Marblehead, Mass – 17 miles from Deer Island.

<u>Anchoring of Lighthouse Beacon- K</u> – "We surround the lighthouse in a circle, moving clockwise and implanting diamond crystals, radiating them outward in every direction through the ley lines of the grid.... connecting them to the crystal prisms in hidden underground caverns of Earth; feel the call and awaken now! We call upon Divine Most High to activate and empower this Beacon with the Sacred Flames of Emanation.   And so it IS!"

<u>Call to the Magical Guardian creatures - J</u> "We call upon the powerful archetypal energies of our brothers and sisters, the magical guardian creatures of the multiverse. Phoenix-finisher, Dragon- creator and protector, Merfolk- holders of the ancient sisterhood power, Feline Familiars- warriors of independence and Sovereignty, Sphynx – Fire Crystal guardians.....we ask that you surround us and bring forth your energies on behalf of the Earth's grid and all life to assist this mission.

Prayer of Protection and Blessings for our friend R.G. - B: (Unscripted)

Unity Vow – J (to focus attention (and Intention) to the shared mission of Unity) "Warriors of divine mission, Guardians of the Sacred Flames, we are Soul Family from across all cosmic nations and creeds, and I call upon you now to Re-Unite in Service to the Earth, in Service to Others, and in Service to Truth! Renew now and sustain the divine light within us all; remember and rededicate to our Sacred Mission. I avow my dedication to our sacred, shared purpose and do not consent to any artificial and inorganic intentions; I release all incoherence back to Source! And So It Is."

**<u>Begin Guided Journey to the Target Locations --
Portal Collapse/Targets - I :</u>**

Numerous technologies have been implanted from the inverted militaristic Saturnian control system to overlay artificial spirals in the organic grid to imprison and destroy the Divine Sophianic Feminine principal; imprisonment of the innocent Indigenous, murder of women, and farmers all connected to Earth Energies, the taking of the land by blood sacrifice; imprisoning the powerful energies of sovereignty, courage and freedom in artificial structures, siphoning the trauma of victimization and fear, and allowing the spread of commercialization to deceive the population. At each location, we will check in with Mother Earth to ensure that we are doing the work that She desires.

- **<u>Winter Island</u>** –   Asking for Divine intervention and assistance to use our loving light Life Force to collapse portal and restore the hijacking of patriarchal control grid overlay of the Military fort Pickering; saturate the land with a blanket of Jesus' Divine Light – and unbind the blood sacrifice of the four on Execution Hill, releasing the trapped spirits back to the light. Activate the Diamond Crystal light gridlines and plant Herkimer diamonds to amplify. Asking for Dragon protection, and the planting of dragon eggs. Relight the Lighthouse beacon with the Eternal Violet Flame and restore the sacred land to sovereign native Naumkeag Tribal stewardship; connect to the two Eternal flames in the lanterns of the North Church in Boston! Speak Ho'oponopono together, thank you, PORTAL IS CLOSED.

- **<u>Deer Island</u>** – (Prison of native Tribal people; now sewage plant) - Asking for Divine intervention and assistance to collapse portals and release the artificial inversions created by the recycling shit and blood sacrifice –channeling the original Krystos frequencies back into the organic grid, and requesting Merfolk and sea creatures to cleanse and purify the land and restore it to the organic Krystos spiral and guard the island; activating the Diamond Crystal light gridlines and planting Herkimer diamonds to amplify. Speak Ho'oponopono together, PORTAL IS CLOSED.

- **<u>Salem Village Meetinghouse and Witchcraft Memorial</u>** (The beginning point; Witchcraft victims accused) Asking for Divine intervention and assistance bringing in the Gold-Violet Flame of cleansing, healing and transmutation to collapse portal and dissolve, and release fear and trauma trapped in the land and held in place by monument and transform it. Assist humanity to integrate the lessons of remorse, responsibility and forgiveness and transform to higher consciousness. Plant Seven-tiered flower of eternal life grid in the earth with pure crystals to activate seven chakras; Tiger eye (root) for grounding, community and safety; carnelian (sacral) for creation and protection of the family-Trinity; citrine quartz (solar plexis)- restoration of sovereign power, aventurine (heart) for love, compassion and luck; blue topaz (throat) to activate the authentic voice and truth; lapis (third eye) for intuition, sacred discernment and connection to higher self and selenite (crown) for connection to Source and Divinity. Speak Ho'onoponopono together, thank you, PORTAL IS CLOSED.

- **<u>Proctors Ledge</u>**- 7 Pope street, Salem; site of hangings. Asking for Divine intervention and assistance to collapse portal and dissolve with the Pink Flame of universal love and forgiveness from the Earth's Heart Chakra, connected to the heart chakras of all beings, releasing trapped soul fragments and consciousnesses of victimization, pain and suffering and transmuting them back to Source. Asking for the Archangels and Guardian Creatures to surround this site and assist to restore the organic, Krystos spiral, radiating out across the Earth's grid and sanctifying this land with Divine purpose, reclaiming it by Earth as a sacred site of Divine feminine power. Planting Herkimer Diamond crystals in thirteen points around the land to magnify and radiate Earth Energy into the grid and out across the land. Speak Ho'oponopono together, thank you, PORTAL IS CLOSED.

- **Old Salem Witch Jail**- (Prison Lane, next to Howard St) - Asking for Divine Intervention and assistance to collapse portal and dissolve, sending the Green Flame of Healing into the land dissolving any remaining anchors, releasing any trapped spirits and channeling organic Krystos frequencies back into the Earth's grid, cleansing and healing. Speak Ho'oponopono together, thank you, PORTAL IS CLOSED.

- **<u>Howard Street Cemetary</u>** – (Giles Corey's execution and burial site- haunting) Asking for Divine intervention and assistance to collapse portals, seal off implant technologies, and channel the organic Krystos frequencies back into the Earth's grid, cleansing and healing the ground with the White Flame of Purification, releasing all trapped soul fragments back to Source with recognition of their highest Divine purpose! Speak Ho'oponopono together, thank you, PORTAL IS CLOSED.

- **<u>House of 7 Gables</u>** (115 Derby St – Nathanial Hathorne house). Asking for Divine intervention and assistance to collapse and seal portals, flooding with the Blue Flame of protection and Divine blessings, sweeping away all ancestral karma, guilt and trauma to allow healing and release of trapped spirits so that they may return

227

to Source! Speak Ho'oponopono together, thank you, PORTAL IS CLOSED.

- **<u>Pickman House</u>** (43 Charter St- haunted house where daughter died tied up/starved in attic, mother was boiled in hot wax). Asking for Divine intervention and assistance to collapse and seal portals, flooding with the Blue Flame of protection and Divine blessings, sweeping away all ancestral karma, guilt and trauma to allow healing and release of trapped spirits so that they may return to Source! Bringing in the Gold Flame to join with the Blue in the Sacred Divine Masculine and Divine Feminine archetypal energies to restore the toxic inversion. Asking for Archangel protection to restore the organic, Krystos spiral and send pure Divine frequency through the grid lines. Speak Ho'oponopono together, thank you, PORTAL IS CLOSED.

- **<u>Masonic Temple</u>** (70 Washington St, Salem – formerly Pickman-Derby mansion) - Asking for

Divine intervention and assistance, collapsing portals and correcting inversion spirals to organic, Krystos frequency. Calling forth the Blue Flame to transform Service-to-Self energies of exploitation, commercialization and greed, and restore Humanity's Sovereign Responsibility as Brother's Keeper consciousness to the land, with Divine Love, protection and blessings. Planting of Dragon Eggs for continued protection. Speak Ho'oponopono together, thank you, PORTAL IS CLOSED.

- **<u>Satanic Temple</u>** (64 bridge street, Salem) - Asking for Divine intervention and assistance, calling forth the Blue Flame to transform Service-to-Self energies of exploitation, commercialization and greed, and restore Sovereign Responsibility as Brother's Keeper consciousness to the land in Divine Love, protection and blessings. Asking for Archangel assistance to free all trapped, tortured souls and assist them to return to Source; planting Dragon Eggs for continued protection. Speak Ho'oponopono together, thank you. PORTAL IS CLOSED.

- **<u>Korn Leather factory</u>**-(57 Boston Street, Salem – start of 1914 fire). Asking for Divine intervention and assistance to pour in the Rainbow Spectrum of Divine Light Ray emanation and amplify and radiate out into the grid, activating the pure Diamond Crystal Light and calling in the Phoenix-finisher to purify all remaining lower consciousnesses and finish the work that the Great Fire attempted to do with Holy Fire of Transformation. Asking for the assistance of the Archangels, the Guardians, the elementals and the Diamond Crystal Light frequency of the grid. Speak Ho'oponopono together, thank you. PORTAL IS CLOSED.
- Now calling on the Plasma Light flames of the Lighthouses and the Old North Church to

amplify their light, calling in the assistance of all interdimensional Soul Family beings in Service-to-o thers to add their intentions to raise the consciousness in Massachusetts, and across all time, space, dimensions and realities. Send the Rainbow Spectrum of Divine Light through all underground tunnels, purifying and cleansing all the way to the muti-dimensional core of Earth, and reverberating through the Star Gates! We revoke all prior assumptions of Consent to Evil, and demand that Our Free Will Be Done, as According to Divine, Universal Law. AND SO IT IS!

Extraction: Return to Lighthouse - K -- Reseal and declaration of closed portals and affirmation of Protection and activation of organic Krystos Frequency flowing through grid and speaking to crystal consciousness all over world, empowering Gratitude prayer; and return home.

Debrief and Discussion: Much better flow this time! The first itinerary was not clear on which sections were informational and which were active; this second mission had more clarity. The team was more comfortable taking on active roles, and we had an idea what to expect now. People reported that they were able to clearly visualize each targeted area and they were also able to experience the whole mission powerfully. Next mission will be targeting the dark triangle Boston down to Newport and Montauk.

<u>Prior to session:</u>

Participants prep prior to session (shield, ground, meditate, hydrate!)
K - Set up sacred space; map of Massachusetts and crystals to lay out
Pictures of each site
Picture of Four Faces of Man

Notes: Mission much smoother than initial, better flow, greater familiarity, and members taking on more active roles.

About the Author

Kenzie Rhodes is a metaphysical practitioner and spiritual coach who lives in Western Massachusetts with her family, and her three little boars. She began working with Earth Energies after a series of unusual events alerted her to her true mission as a Gridworker, and a Gridwork Facilitator.

She created the Crystal Grid Fairies, a series of books to serve as a Lighthouse for young lightworkers, who came here for a different reason, with the help of her illustrator daughter, Athena who can draw just about anything.

kayazuray@yahoo.com

Kay's website: www.crystalgridearthenergyhealing.com

www.ingramcontent.com/pod-product-compliance
Lightning Source LLC
Chambersburg PA
CBHW051820150726

47998CB00001B/223